THE GREEK
ORTHODOX
CHURCH

THE GREEK ORTHODOX CHURCH--By

Panagiotis Bratsiotis

Translated by Joseph Blenkinsopp

UNIVERSITY OF NOTRE DAME PRESS--Notre Dame--London

EDITOR'S FOREWORD

DR. PANAGIOTIS BRATSIOTIS, a Greek Orthodox Christian deeply committed to his Church, a theologian of international fame and well-known author (according to a count taken in 1955 he had fifty-five scientific publications to his credit), is a biblical scholar attached to the theological faculty of Athens University. As member and for some years president of the Athenian Academy of the Sciences, as representative of his country in important international organizations, and as participant in theological and ecumenical congresses of great historical significance, he has brought great honor to his native land. As is the case with all theology professors in both Greek universities (the second, that of Salonika, was founded in this century) Bratsiotis is not an ordained priest. He is a lay theologian. The Greek Church has never known a laity inferior to the clergy or a rift between clergy and laity as was the case in the Catholic Middle Ages in both southern and northern Europe. In the Greek Church male worshippers do not mill about the doors or in the vestibule of the church, with the front seats all taken by the women. They find their place up front near the ikonostasis and are not afraid to take part in the singing of those ancient hymns that Bratsiotis speaks of in the first and fourth chapters of his book. Anyone taking part in the liturgy in a small Greek town can also see how, after the reading of the gospel, the celebrant will go to his place and a teacher of religion from the secondary school will go to the ambo and give the sermon. This is explained by the fact that while the latter will have done a full course in theology, the former may only have gone through the ordinary practical and ascetical training given in the seminary.

In terms of official status in the Church, Bratsiotis is a layman, but he is no layman as far as theology is concerned. He has made a significant contribution to the investigation of the Old and New Testament, as the titles of his published works show. In 1928 he brought out a study on the pilgrim songs of the Psalter, in 1937 an introduction to the Old Testament, and in 1949 a commentary on the Apocalypse. These works earned him the recognition of well-known biblical theologians and reviews in the best journals by both Catholics and Protestants, for example, O. Eissfeldt, O. Procksch, F. Stier, F. Zorell, and J. Bonsirven. Pierre Benoit attested that his work was a credit to modern Greek exegesis. In addition, Bratsiotis was already deeply

engaged in political and social problems such as socialism and the
movement for women's rights. A good part of his energy and efforts
was taken up in ecumenical work, and he made a close study of
Anglicanism and the dialectic theology of Karl Barth and Emil
Brunner. After Germany, where he did his theological studies, he was
specially attached to England, Scotland, and Belgium. He proved his
attachment to Germany by sending his son, now Dr. Nicholas Bratsiotis, instructor at the University of Athens, to continue his Old
Testament studies in that country, at the theological faculty of Munich.

In view of all this it will be readily understood that any kind of
narrow-mindedness is foreign to the nature of Bratsiotis. Yet his
ecumenism is based more on brotherly love than theological depth of
thinking. The reader may have had the same experience as Catholic
Christians in other European countries, of having learned in school
that hardly anything separates us from Greek Christians (basically
only the different approach to the Roman primacy) and of thinking
that reunion with the Greeks was a formality (merely a question of an
intelligent approach by the leading men of both sides), and then of
finding out when he looks more closely that the Greeks like all Orthodox Christians, are characterized above all by a deeply rooted sense
of independence. They are determined, come what may, to hold on to
this independence, especially in the ecclesiastical and theological
spheres. One does not often find the Greeks making concessions in
ecumenical or theological discussions, to the extent that experienced
ecumenical theologians would be inclined to say that in all probability
reunion between Constantinople and Rome would not be the first
step toward the Great Church of the future.

Panagiotis Bratsiotis is also a conservative thinker. That love for
the truth which is characteristic of the Greeks prevents him from
covering in discreet silence the things that separate him, as a Greek,
from us. But it also leads him to confess with passionate conviction
the things that unite him with us. This book has the character of a
personal confession of faith. It is marked by a clearly defined and
all-inclusive piety. It conveys at the same time the courage involved
in a deeply rooted faith and the wisdom which the experience of a
long lifetime has brought.

GÜNTER STACHEL
Editor

PREFACE

THE DECREE on Ecumenism of the Second Vatican Council has a section entitled "The Special Position of the Eastern Churches" which emphasizes their great importance: "All should realize that it is of supreme importance to understand, venerate, preserve, and foster the exceedingly rich liturgical and spiritual heritage of the Eastern Churches, in order faithfully to preserve the fullness of Christian tradition, and to bring about reconciliation between Eastern and Western Christians" (Art. 15). From this we can see how the Council honors and respects the individual position of the Eastern Churches and their illustrious history. Their history is one of unbroken fidelity to the Gospel and the apostolic traditions, in the cause of which Eastern Christians have witnessed in spite of the severest trials and persecutions and even martyrdom. The Council speaks of the liturgical and spiritual tradition of Eastern Christians with the greatest respect, love, and reverence. Pride of place is given in this tradition to the celebration of the Eucharist, but there is also the veneration of Mary and the saints and the splendid hymns which go with it, monasticism, the veneration of icons, Eastern canon law, and a highly characteristic theology which often brings out certain aspects of the revealed Mystery more clearly than in Western theology. In fact we can say that Eastern and Western theology complement each other in a very felicitous way. It is the merit of Professor Bratsiotis' work that he has brought out clearly the ecumenical significance of the *one* apostolic deposit of faith contained in Scripture and tradition.

What the Council document only describes in outline or merely alludes to will be found in all its richness and fullness in the present work of the eminent and ecumenically minded Greek Orthodox professor of theology, Panagiotis Bratsiotis. At the same time, he does not pass over in silence the obstacles which still stand in the way of full unity between the Churches.

The removal of the mutual excommunication of 1054 is a very hopeful sign that the wall of division will eventually disappear. Both Pope Paul VI together with the Council Fathers and Patriarch Athenagoras with his synod were conscious of the fact that this act of mutual reparation and forgiveness would not in itself remove the differences which existed between the two bodies. These can only be overcome "by the operation of the Holy Spirit leading to a purification of hearts, repentance for the injustice done throughout history, and a real determination to arrive at a common understanding and expression of apostolic faith and its demands." After this declaration had been read in the Council, the choir sang the liturgical text "Ubi caritas et amor, Deus ibi est," and all joined in with a glad heart.

CARDINAL LORENZ JAEGER
Archbishop of Paderborn Germany

INTRODUCTION

THE AUTHOR of this book was invited as a representative of a leading Christian Church to express himself on that Church. The purpose of this invitation was in full accord with the widely conceived and pioneering aims of the great father of the Second Vatican Council, Pope John XXIII of happy memory, to whom unfortunately it was not granted to see the seed which he had sown ripen into the harvest. Αἰωνία αὐτου ἡ μνήμη . . . and in truth his memory will remain alive throughout the whole Church forever. *Memoria eius in generationem et generationem.*

I wish to express my thanks to the publishers and the editor of this book for giving me the opportunity of sharing in this work. As far as my contribution is concerned, the following points are basic throughout:

1. The basic principle enunciated in the invitation which I received: "Interconfessional dialogue will always break down where there is a lack of understanding of what makes Christians of other confessions the kind of Christians they are."

2. Love of my Church and for the truth.

3. Concern and love for all other Churches.

This same basic attitude was behind my two-volume work entitled *Die Orthodoxe Kirche in griechischer Sicht,* which the Protestant Evangelical publishing house of Stuttgart asked me to write and published in 1959 and 1960 and which was well received by the public.

At the editor's request this contribution will also be concerned with giving a personal presentation. Though it has not been too easy for me, I have attempted to express myself more in a personal and even autobiographical way. I pray God to place his seal upon this effort of a lay theologian made after fifty years service to his Church, and I beg the reader, whether Orthodox Christian or not, for his kind indulgence.

PANAGIOTIS BRATSIOTIS

CONTENTS

THE GREEK
ORTHODOX
CHURCH

MY LIFE

I WAS BORN in Thebes in 1889, the only child of pious Orthodox parents. My father was a married priest; he ministered first in Thebes, and from 1901 to 1935, the year of his death, in the church of St. Constantine in Athens, the foundation stone of which had been laid by the then only five-year-old Crown Prince Constantine, who later became king. My father had studied at a junior ecclesiastical seminary and therefore had no real scientific theological education. He was, however, full of zeal for his Church and as a priest totally dedicated to his sacred ministry. He thus gave me a good grounding in Orthodox faith.

My Studies in Greece

For five years I attended the oldest and largest ecclesiastical seminary in Greece, Rizarios Seminary in Athens, which had been founded in 1844, shortly after the liberation of the country, by the pious brothers Rizaris from Epirus, who had grown rich in Russia. Most of the pupils had scholarships; for the most part they came from the provinces which had been in the hands of the Turks until 1913—Epirus, Macedonia, Thrace, the Asia Minor province, Crete, Cyprus, the Aegean Islands, and the Dodecanese. After completing their studies, they went back to their native provinces and worked there as priests and teachers.

In this seminary which was, as I have indicated, a Panhellenic school, I had the good fortune, together with many other present-day professors and bishops, of receiving a fine education in theology and the humanities from theologians and philologists of solid standing. The seminary was under the direction of Nektarios Kephalas, the former metropolitan of Pentapolis in the Alexandrian Patriarchate, a highly skilled and well-known theologian who, however, left the seminary as early as 1908 to found a monastery in the island of Aegina in order to dedicate himself to a life of asceticism. He died in 1920 in the odor of sanctity and four years ago was officially canonized by the ecumenical patriarch.[1] I also had the opportunity in this seminary to become acquainted with Byzantine church music through John Sakelaridis, a well-known master and composer, the former *protopsaltes* or precentor of the cathedral of Athens. He always impressed on his students how important Byzantine hymnography was in their

1. Patriarch of Constantinople (Istanbul) (editor's note).

3

dogmatic and, in general, theological training. I owe to him my first love and admiration for the great treasure of the Byzantine liturgy.

In 1907, at the conclusion of my studies in Rizarios Seminary, I matriculated in the theological faculty of the University of Athens. This university had been founded in 1837 by the first Greek king, the good Otto I, a son of the great philhellene Ludwig I of Bavaria, and had been set up on the model of a German university. I studied theology for four years and at the same time took classes in philosophy, history, and classical philology in the faculty of philosophy.

I may be permitted to add that while I was studying at the university, I also sang in the choir of Saint Constantine, the parish church of my father, together with other theological students. This involved not only the liturgy of the Mass but also Vespers and Lauds, and the singing was conducted by the *protopsaltes* John Sakelaridis, whom I have already mentioned. And so in the course of time I acquired a good knowledge of the treasure of Byzantine hymnology, so rich in theological content, which this widely read and enthusiastic teacher explained to us in the light of the Greek Fathers and also, as occasion demanded, of classical authors.

For the most part my professors of theology had studied in the Protestant faculties of German universities. They all remained true to the teachings of their church but did not have a very friendly attitude toward the Roman Catholic Church—not even that minority of them who had studied at Roman Catholic universities. This anti-Roman feeling can be explained, on the one hand, in the light of a sad, centuries-long tradition in Orthodoxy, on the other, by the anti-Orthodox attitude evident in Roman Catholic theology at that time.

I thank God that, to some extent at least, I managed to maintain a certain independence in the midst of this tense, anti-Roman atmosphere. By means of certain lectures and books suggested for reading by my professors I was able to become familiar with many of the good aspects of the Roman Catholic Church: its mystical tradition, many of its saints and its great theologians and reformers. On the great feast days I often used to visit the Basilica of Saint Denis,[2] which in that year was celebrating its centenary jubilee. The music of the Catholic liturgy was very much to my taste, and I was so enthused by the playing of the organ that I bought myself a harmonium on which I played Orthodox and Western church music.

Apart from the reading of the Greek fathers, I was early attracted

2. The cathedral of the Roman Catholic bishop of Athens (editor's note).

by a great number of Latin and French authors. While still in the
Rizarios Seminary I had read Lactantius, Ambrose, Jerome, Fénelon,
and Bossuet. While a student at Athens University I read the *Confessions* of Saint Augustine as well as many of the Latin ascetical
authors of the Middle Ages, especially the *Imitation of Christ* of
Thomas a Kempis. My interest in ascetical writings stemmed from the
fact that from quite an early age I was occupied with the problems
of self-knowledge and self-discipline, and this without any knowledge at all of Western psychological theories. I must attribute this
tendency in myself to good confessors, in particular Father Eusebius
Mathopoulos, the founder of *Zoé* [Life], the well-known association
of theologians. While still a student of theology I took part in his
biblical seminars.

STUDIES ABROAD

When I had finished my studies at the University of Athens, I had
to make up my mind at which German university I should continue
in order to deepen my knowledge of philosophy and theology. I decided for Leipzig, since it then had a good name in theology and
philosophy, and, moreover, I had there a valuable friend, Theologos
Paraskewaidis, the former deacon of my father at the church of Saint
Constantine in Athens who was by now the archimandrate of the
Greek community in Leipzig, one of the first of such communities to
be established on German soil. I owe him a debt of gratitude for the
guidance and encouragement he gave me in my studies and my
personal life. He was at that time my mentor and father-confessor,
and I helped him out with the singing in his church.

In Leipzig I lived with my mother at Querstrasse 27, quite close
to the Greek church and the university. Since I already knew German
I could get on at once with the task of deepening my knowledge of
exegesis, philosophy, and pedagogy. In October, 1912, I matriculated
in the faculty of philosophy and followed the lectures of many well-
known teachers including W. Wundt, E. Spranger, J. Volkelt, R. Kittel,
G. Heinrici, H. Guthe, C. R. Gregory, and the famous Swedish historian of religions, Nathan Söderblom, later to become Archbishop
of Uppsala, who was then visiting-professor at Leipzig. In addition,
I also took part in the seminar on problems of the Septuagint[3] directed
by H. Windisch, then instructor at the university.

3. The Septuagint is the Greek translation of the Old Testament which originated
in the third and second centuries B.C.

I later continued my studies at Jena, where I followed the lectures of the theologians Staerk, Wendt, Weinel, Lietzmann, Haas, the philosopher Eucken, and the educationalist Rein. Philosophy and education were necessary for my future work as teacher in educational institutes, but I learned a great deal from them for my theological work in general.

My special interest was in the history of religions, which then played a great part in theological and biblical studies. My teachers Heinrici and Kittel warned their students with all possible emphasis against applying indiscriminately the methods of the history of religion in biblical studies, and I was so taken up with these questions that I published one of my first essays as early as 1920 under the title *Die sogenannte religionsgeschichtliche Schule* ("The So-called School of the History of Religions"). During that critical period for theology in the West, when an all-out, disastrous liberalism and historicism was inducing doubts and uncertainties of conscience on all sides, I was able to make my way clear by means of the single-minded approach taught me by my parents, my teachers in Athens, and, later, my professors at Leipzig. At the same time I discovered the valuable contribution of Roman Catholic biblical and religious studies, and, despite the fact that I had never studied at a Catholic faculty, my sympathy with the Roman Catholic Church grew all the time. This was strengthened later when I became more closely associated with Catholic professors in exegetical studies. At the same time I learned a great deal from Protestant biblical studies. I followed in this respect the advice of the Apostle, "test everything; hold fast what is good" (1 Thess. 5:21), and allowed myself to be guided by the example of Gregory of Nazianzen and Basil the Great. As is well known, the latter wrote a treatise entitled "How can the young derive profit from the writings of the pagans?"

THE MAIN PRINCIPLES
WHICH INSPIRED MY STUDIES

Perhaps I may, at this point, say something briefly on what has inspired my studies throughout. My theological work has been guided by the love for truth and knowledge, the love of my people, and, above all, love for my Church. It was the Church which first led me to study theology, and even though I did not become a minister of the Church in the strict sense of the term, I have, as the son of a priest, as a professor of theology and of the teachings of the Church, to thank her for everything.

In the course of my life I have made acquaintance with people from many nations, yet this has only helped me to love my own people more. Similarly, my acquaintance with other Churches has helped me to know, treasure, and love my own Church that much more. I can even say that it was love for my Church which led me to study theology, and yet, despite the fact that I was the son of a priest, I remained a layman. All this will explain why I wished to dedicate to my Church all my love and zeal and serve her in all things without any kind of reserve.

THE COURSE OF MY THEOLOGICAL WORK

I should now say something about the course which my theological work has taken. When I came back to Greece I had to do my military service. For me the army was not only a good education from the social point of view; it also presented me with a missionary task. I was given the task by my company commander to preach every week to the troops, and from time to time I also gave, at the request of my divisional commander, some talks on religious themes. The army provided me with the opportunity of mixing with men from every social level of our people, and in this way I could acquire a better idea of their strong and weak points.

After my military service had come to an end, I was appointed professor of religion, philosophy, and pedagogy at the teacher-training college of the Piraeus and later at that of Athens. I recall this period of my life very well since it was my first appointment and I had the opportunity of furthering my methodological and theological education. The teaching experience which this provided me with and the important themes I was handling played a great part in broadening my spiritual horizons. I was, however, left with enough free time to continue my systematic study of the Bible, though I was twice snatched away from my work by a military draft in those dark years of the First World War. Nevertheless I succeeded in completing my doctoral dissertation and in 1918 was granted a doctorate from the theological faculty of Athens University. In 1924 I was appointed instructor in New Testament studies and in November, 1925, named associate professor of biblical history. In the semesters of the years 1925 to 1928 I lectured on questions concerning the history of Old and New Testament times and explained the Psalms in the Greek version. In 1928 I was given the additional task of taking over the introduction to the Old Testament.

On the basis of my studies in the Septuagint I was appointed in 1929 as full professor in the newly established chair of Old Testament introduction and exegesis of the Septuagint. My good friend and former teacher Professor Hans Lietzmann wrote to me to express his joy at my appointment and the establishment of this new chair, and his conviction that the Septuagint, as "the Bible of the Orthodox, as it was of the primitive Church," must have a special importance for the Christian understanding of the Old Testament.

This is perhaps the best point at which to explain the procedure involved in the appointment of a professor to a theological faculty in our country. According to the Greek view the Orthodox Church is the official state-church, yet the Holy Synod has no say in the choice of a theology professor; this is the exclusive right of the theological faculties of the universities concerned. This academic freedom does not, however, imply that the Holy Synod has no right to take an interest in what is being taught in matters of faith in a theological faculty. After all, it is there that the Orthodox clergy and the teachers responsible for obligatory scholastic instruction in Orthodoxy are educated. My purpose here is simply to give a clear idea of the legal status of the synod, since in practice all of the professors of our two theological faculties[4] feel themselves under the obligation to keep the promise which they made before the assembled faculty and in the presence of the rector of the university when they received their doctorates, a promise which involves "loyal adhesion to the dogmas of the Orthodox Church on the basis of holy Scripture and the decisions of the seven ecumenical councils." It is not, however, only this solemn promise made by the doctor of theology which obligates him to loyalty toward his spiritual mother but also his own personal faith and a feeling of gratitude and devotion. This acknowledgment of the fact that our Church has widespread obligations and an important service to perform on behalf of believers, together with the acute consciousness that the scientific means for fulfilling her task are always inadequate, explains why I too felt obliged to take on myself so much work concerned with scientific biblical study and spiritual problems.

My interest as a theological writer was directed in the first place toward biblical studies, which take up the greater part of my published work. I give here a list of titles:

4. In 1942 the University of Thessalonica was completed.

Die politischen Verhältnisse des Judentums im Zeitalter Jesu Christi ("The Political Connections of Judaism at the Time of Jesus Christ"), 1918.

Das israelitisch-jüdische Erziehungs- und Schulwesen ("The Hebrew and Jewish System of Education and Teaching"), 1920.

Die sogenannte religionsgeschichtliche Schule ("The So-called History of Religions School"), 1920.

Johannes der Täufer als Prophet ("John the Baptist as Prophet"), 1921.

Kommentar zum Philemonbrief mit einem Anhang über die Sklaverei im Altertum und im Christentum ("A Commentary on the Epistle to Philemon with an Appendix on Slavery in the Ancient World and in Christianity"), 1923.

Der "Am haarez" in den Evangelien ("The 'People of the Land' in the Gospels"), 1924.

Die Parabeln des Herrn und die moderne Kritik ("The Parables of The Lord and Modern Criticism"), 1924.

Die Sprache der Septuaginta ("The Language of the Septuagint"), 1925.

Paulus und die Septuaginta ("Paul and the Septuagint"), 1925.

Die Frau in der Bible ("Woman in the Bible"), 1925, 1938.[2]

Die Philister und die ägäokretische Kultur ("The Philistines and the Civilization of the Aegean and Crete"), 1925.

Die soziale Bedeutung des Alten Testaments ("The Social Significance of the Old Testaments"), 1938, 1953.[2]

Kommentar zu den Stufenpsalmen ("A Commentary on the Psalms of Ascent"), 1928, 1956.[2]

Einleitung in das Alte Testament ("Introduction to the Old Testament"), 1937, 1956.[2]

Kommentar zur Johannesapokalypse ("A Commentary on the Apocalypse of St. John"), 1949.

Kommentar zum Ekklesiastes ("A Commentary on Ecclesiastes"), 1953.

Kommentar zu Jesaja ("A Commentary on Isaiah"), 1956.

Der Sinn der christlichen Agape ("The Meaning of Christian Agape"), 1956.

My work in the ecumenical movement and my interest in the revival of theology in the West after the First World War brought me in contact with Karl Barth, the leading figure in dialectic theology, and Emil Brunner, the other great representative of this movement. I found, among other things in their writings, a reaction against the liberalism and historicism of the period before the war. Out of my interest in Barthian theology there grew a small publication (1930). In 1935 I published another on the theology of Emil Brunner, and five years later there appeared my study of his Christian anthropology.

Being an official representative of my Church at ecumenical and, more recently, Pan-Orthodox conferences forced on me an intensive concern with dogmatic theology, ethics, liturgy, the history of the Orthodox Church, the teaching of the Fathers, and, lastly, with theology as it was developing in other parts of the world. On these themes I published the following short studies and essays:

Die Grundprinzipien und Hauptmerkmale der Orthodoxen Kirche ("The Basic Principles and Chief Characteristics of the Orthodox Church"), in German, 1938.

"Staat-Nation-Kirche" ("State-Nation-Church") in *Zeitschrift für Internationale Theologie,* Berne, 1936.

"Das Menschenverständnis der Orthodoxen Kirche" ("The Orthodox Church's Understanding of Man") in *Theologische Zeitschrift,* Basle, 1950.

"Die Autorität der Bibel in der Orthodoxen Kirche heute" ("The Authority of the Bible in the Orthodox Church Today") in *Die Autorität der Bibel heute,* a publication of the World Council of Churches which appeared in German and English.

"Paulus und die Einheit der Kirche" ("Paul and the Unity of the Church") in *Studia Paulina in honorem Johannis de Zwaan,* 1953.

Apostle Paul and the Orthodox Church (The Festival Volume of the 1900th Anniversary of St. Paul's Arrival in Greece, 1953).

Griechentum und Christentum in Synthese und Antithese ("Greek Civilization and Christianity in Synthesis and Antithesis"), inaugural dissertation on being admitted to the Athenian Academy, 1957.

"Die Theosislehre der Orthodoxen Kirche" ("The Teaching on Theosis in the Orthodox Church"), Mededelingen van de Koninklijke Vlaamse Akademie, Klasse der Letteren, 1961.

Die Orthodoxe Kirche in griechischer Sicht, Vol. I, 1959, pp. 208 ff; Vol. II, 1960, pp. 192 ff (published, in collaboration with other Greek theologians as the first volume of a collection entitled *Die Kirchen der Welt,* by the Evangelical publishing house of Stuttgart).

As a full member of the Academy of Sciences from 1955 I took part in its research work. The theme of my inaugural dissertation dealt with "Greek Civilization and Christianity in Synthesis and Antithesis" (see above). In November, 1959, I represented the academy in the capacity of vice-rector at the celebration of the bicentenary of the founding of the Bavarian Academy of Sciences. In 1960 I became rector of the academy and took as my inaugural theme "Technology and Technocracy Seen from the Christian Point of View." In April, 1963, I delivered an address to the academy for the thousandth anniversary of the founding of monasticism on Mount Athos and spoke of the significance of this holy place both for the Orthodox Church and the Greek people in general.

I wrote two small works to combat liberal tendencies in recent Greek theology. In 1931 there appeared *Autorität und Freiheit in der Orthodoxen Theologie* ("Authority and Freedom in Orthodox Theology") and in 1948 *Die griechische Theologie in den letzen fünfzig Jahren* ("Greek Theology in the Last Fifty Years"). I also took issue with humanist, antichristian movements of thought in *Christentum und Kultur* ("Christianity and Culture"), 1940; *Christentum und Humanismus* ("Christianity and Humanism"), 1955; and *Christentum und Technik* ("Christianity and Technology"), 1960.

Together with other colleagues and scholars in widely different fields of specialization I organized the first congress for Greek-Christian culture during the time when I was rector of the university, in May, 1956. This congress was chaired by the great Greek physician Professor M. Gerulanos, and the acts were published in Athens in 1957.

I had been interested in social questions since 1923, and I have expressed the Christian point of view in many publications: *Die Frau in der Bibel* ("Woman in the Bible"), 1922; *War Christus Sozialist?* ("Was Christ a Socialist?"), 1925; *Christentum und Sozialismus im westlichen Europa* ("Christianity and Socialism in West Europe"), 1931; *Die drei grossen griechischen Hierarchen und die soziale Frage* ("The Three Great Greek Patriarchs and the Social Question"), an academic address delivered in 1930; *Die Theologie der Arbeit bei den griechischen Kirchenvätern* ("The Theology of Work in the Greek Fathers of the Church"), an academic address delivered in 1959; *Christentum und Arbeit* ("Christianity and Work"), a paper read at the celebration of the first of the Workers' Sundays organized by the Church in 1960. I succeeded in obtaining the cooperation of Professor A. Kousis and Privy Councillor P. Poulitsas in introducing the Christian-socialist movement into Greece and founding the Christian-Socialist Union in 1932. On the initiative of Kousis, a medical practitioner, an anticancer research institute was built with state aid, which today consists of a hospital with 350 beds, the most up-to-date equipment for treatment, and a research institute. Early work in Christian-socialism was carried on by the Christian-Socialist Union, to which many Christian sociologists and politicians belong today, among them President Stephan Stephanopoulos and several university professors.

Early in my career I had been attracted to working in a Christian way with university students. It was from this activity that the two Greek Christian student movements were derived; these maintain contact with the Christian World Union of Students and the ecumenical and pan-Orthodox youth movement "Syndesmos."

Ever since 1921, when the Holy Synod entrusted me with the editorship of the then official ecclesiastical review *Hieros Syndesmos*,[5] I have taken part in church work in the real sense of the term. Since 1923 I shared in the redaction of the theological journal *Theologia*, founded by Chrysostomos Papadopoulos, Archbishop of Athens. From 1937 to 1941 I was one of those responsible for the bibliographical supplement of the review *Theologische Literaturzeitung*. Since 1951 I have been a member of the Society for New Testament Studies (Societas Studiorum Novi Testamenti), and was one of the four main speakers, together with Dodd, Bultmann, and Clavier, at its annual congress in Berne in 1952. The theme of the congress was the anthropology of the new Testament. I was also on the editorial board of the international journal *Novum Testamentum* when it was launched. The last twenty-five years of my life have been full of work for church unity, about which I shall have something to say later.

A great number of professors from the theological faculties of Athens and Thessalonica have taken part with me in ecclesiastical and social work. It would not be wrong to say that the theological faculty of the national university of Athens constitutes a permanent advisory board for the Holy Synod, and on more than one occasion its opinion has been solicited on some theological question and the results of its investigations placed before the Synod. At the same time, this faculty has given to the autocephalous Church of Greece three bishops and three primates from the time of its foundation to the present.

5. Greek for "holy union."

A GLANCE AT THE HISTORY OF THE ORTHODOX CHURCH

1. THE ORTHODOX CHURCH understands itself to be the genuine continuation of the undivided, ancient, and catholic Church formed by the primitive faith in the Resurrection. As a result of the disastrous schism which began in the year 867 and was completed in 1054, it was separated from the Church of the West. But already in the period of the undivided Church, the Church of the "new" or "second" Rome, as it was called to distinguish it from the Church of ancient Rome, had certain basic characteristics:

a. It is essentially theoretical, ascetical, and mystical, in contrast to the practical spirit of the Roman Church.

b. Its general character, in particular as regards language and culture, is Greek, whereas Rome and the West in general, despite the diffusion of Greek thinking, remain essentially Latin. Here the achievement of Rome in civilizing some of the Germanic peoples played an important part.

c. In the East there exist many apostolic Churches which are autonomous and keep their own traditions. In the West, on the contrary, there is only one apostolic Church and therefore only *one* supreme ecclesiastical authority, which is the Church of Rome. The bishop of Rome is the vehicle of the tradition and the supreme authority in the Church. As opposed to this concentration of authority in the Western Church, we in the East have a democratic, synodal, and federal church organization.

d. Whereas the Eastern Churches manifest strong mystical tendencies (Simeon the Theologian, Nicholas Karbasilas, Gregory Palamas), Aristotelianism, on which the Thomistic system is built, made great progress in the West.

A very strong characteristic of our Church is its fidelity to tradition.

These differences already existed centuries before the Schism and in the course of time became even greater. The estrangement between

13

the two parts of the Universal Church became permanent after the division.

In the Gospel of John (19:23) we read of the symbolic prophecy of the Lord's seamless robe. This robe has been torn, and Church leaders, together with the faithful entrusted to them, now have the task of restoring that heavenly garment to its former perfection. The West tried continually to place all the responsibility for the division on the shoulders of the Greek Church at the time of the Macedonian and Commene dynasties, but in doing so forgot that even the deadly enemies of hellenized Byzantium—Slavs, Arabs, and other racial groups— remained true nevertheless to their ecclesiastical tradition.

2. The schism happened at a time which was critical not only for Byzantium but also for the whole Christian world. Attacks from non-Christian peoples threatened on every side. Some, like the Slavs, accepted Christianity, while others, like the Arabs and various Turkish races, inspired by a terrible religious fanaticism, extirpated Christianity in the Near East, Asia, and Africa. The expansion of Islam resulted in the decline of the patriarchates of Antioch, Jerusalem, and Alexandria, and the Greek culture which went with them. Many historians of note have stressed the catastrophic effects of this decisive weakening of the Hellenistic East.

At the beginning of the eighth century the Arabs obtained a foothold in the Iberian Peninsula and threatened the whole of Western Europe. It has long been recognized that the Franks, who saved the West, would not have been able to meet this danger if Byzantium, fortified by its Chrisitan faith, had not put up so strong a resistance to Islam.

3. A significant counter to the tragic loss sustained by the Orthodox Church and its Greco-Christian culture was the evangelization of the Slavs, Rumanians, and Walachians initiated by Patriarch Photius and carried out by Greek monks. The new Orthodox Churches, which were national and autocephalous in character, took enthusiastically to Christianity and Greco-Chrisitan culture and gave their peoples a new unity by means of Greek culture and the Greek language. Despite their national independence, however, they remained dependent on the mother church in Constantinople for the direction of their spiritual life. From her they took not only a culture formed by Hellenism and Chrisitanity but also their spiritually, ecclesiastical tradition, theology, and liturgy. The Ecumenical Patriarchate[1] recognized the autonomy of

1. Patriarchate of Constantinople (editor's note).

the national churches of Serbia (1219), Bulgaria (1235), and Russia (1498). It is, however, significant and characteristic that all the auto- cephalous Churches of the Balkans placed themselves under the pro- tection of the Ecumenical Patriarchate during the time of the Turkish occupation which began in the fourteenth century and ended with the liberation at the end of the nineteenth century. It is not always suffi- ciently recognized how great the contribution of this patriarchate was in this difficult period with regard to the faith of these peoples, the promotion of the liturgy, the formation of their national conscious- ness and the various constitutions which enshrined it, the development of their national languages and of Hellenic-Christian civilization.

The Ecumenical Patriarchate gave assistance and support to the Russian Church when it was threatened by Tartars and Poles. In 1588 the Patriarch Jeremias II, known in the West through his exchange of correspondence with Lutheran theologians and philologists of Tübingen, founded the Russian Patriarchate of Moscow.

4. We can outline the relations of the Orthodox with the Roman Church after the schism as follows: in the thirteenth and fifteenth centuries important attempts were made to reunite the two during the time of the Palaeologi (the Synod of Lyons, 1274; Synods of Ferrara and Florence, 1438–1489). All these attempts, however, failed, since, on the side of the Orthodox at least, they sprang not from a genuine inner conviction on the part of the people, the emperor, and bishops, but rather from political considerations, namely, the menace of the Turks.[2] It was this common danger which explained why the different peoples that had embraced Orthodoxy continued to regard the Ecu- menical Patriarchate as their spiritual mother in spite of national and political differences and tendencies which often went against Byzan- tium and its Greek culture.

From the time of the schism there have been many mutual contacts between East and West. Some of these have been of a cultural nature, while others have consisted in points of agreement or disagreement between Orthodox, Roman Catholic, and Protestant theologians. Visits have been exchanged, Orthodox thought has been studied in the West, and important works have been translated.

There have also been Greek and Slav students who have affiliated

2. I have expressed my personal view on this subject in a review of an important book by Father Joseph Gill, rector of the Pontificio Instituto Orientale, entitled *The Council of Florence* (Cambridge, 1959). The review appeared in Θεολογία I (1963), pp. 166–168.

with the Roman Church, and even some Orthodox clergy. These trans-
fers of allegiance have usually taken place at Western universities and
have been sporadic by nature, brought about either by pressure from
the other side, proselytizing, or poverty. The great mass of the Orthodox faithful, at least as far as the Greeks are concerned, remained
true to their mother church even in territories which for centuries had
been ruled by Roman Catholic leaders.

5. The attempts made by Bohemia and Moravia on the one side and
the Ecumenical Patriarchate on the other to come to an understanding
in 1451, two years before the fall of Constantinople, were without
success. Under Patriarch Photius, Greek missionaries had begun to
preach the faith to these countries. Contacts between the Ecumenical
Patriarchate and the Protestants, especially the Lutherans who in the
first years after the Reformation had tried to reach an understanding
with the Orthodox Church, met the same fate. In the mid-sixteenth
century the Ecumenical Patriarch Joasaph (1556–1565) had sent his
deacon Demetrios Mysos to Wittenburg to obtain more precise infor-
mation on the Reformation, and Melanchthon himself took this
opportunity of sending the Patriarch a long and detailed letter. A few
years later there occurred the famous exchange of correspondence
between the Tübingen professors Jacob Andreas and Martin Crusius
on the one hand and the Ecumenical Patriarch Jeremias II on the
other.[3] Reading these letters today, one wants to ask how it was possible in those dark and fearful days of Turkish rule and spiritual
oppression to write such theological letters. The Orthodox Church
believes that it was only through the help of God that the faith could
have been preserved in such difficult circumstances. We can well understand the pride of that patriarch who wrote to Professor D. Chytraeus:
"Although our people lie in bondage they have not fallen into godless-
ness and continue to sing his praise."[4]

6. Occurring simultaneously with these contacts at a high level
there were strenuous attempts by both Catholics and Protestants to
make converts among the Orthodox. In the course of the sixteenth century the Catholics had considerable success in Poland, southern Italy,
and Sicily, also in Syria, Lebanon, and southwest Russia, mostly in the
form of direct annexation to Roman Catholicism. Apart from some
converts here and there, they had, however, no success among the

3. See J. Karmiris, *Orthodoxy und Protestantism*, 1937 (in Greek); G. Zachariades,
Tübingen und Konstantinopel, 1941; E. Benz, *Byzanz und Wittenburg*, 1949.
4. D. Chytraeus, *Oratio de statu Ecclesiarum in Graecia*, 1580, p. 63.

Greeks, no more than Protestant propaganda in the seventeenth century, which, like that of Rome, went so far as to seek support from foreign diplomats.

The general synods of Constantinople (1640), Iasi in Rumania (1641), and Jerusalem (1672), especially the efforts of the Patriarch of Jerusalem Dositheos († 1707) had done much to clarify and strengthen Orthodox faith in the seventeenth century. Apart from divine providence and the superhuman efforts of the pastors and teachers of the Orthodox Churches, this has to be attributed first and foremost to the fact that the Orthodox world held fast to its dogmatic and liturgical tradition and reacted sharply against any innovation. We can go so far as to say that even those peoples who lived on the perimeter of the Orthodox world and had to suffer under the harsh rule of the foreigner came out of this trial strengthened in faith and moral probity. The fate of the peoples and Churches of the East at this time, Orthodox and otherwise, reminds us of the Babylonian exile of the Jewish people. They, like the Jews, came through their trial without wavering in their attachment to the faith of their fathers or mixing with the heathen.

We can find a very apposite symbol for the part the Church must play in the life of the peoples in the ark of Noah. We can say with justice that this is particularly so in the case of the Orthodox Church, since she brought the peoples of the Balkans, Asia Minor, and the islands of the eastern Mediterranean safely through the countless tempests they have met with in their national history. In its universal role as mother church the Patriarchate of Constantinople was recognized not only by its own peoples but also by the sultans as "the glory of all the enslaved peoples"—all those, that is, who lived within the boundaries of what had once been the Eastern Roman Empire. I may be permitted to quote here from the well-known Bulgarian theologian Stephen Zankow:

The Orthodox Patriarchate of Constantinople was the mother Church of and the model for all European Orthodox Churches. Right down to recent times this patriarchate has played a supportive and leading role with regard to the Eastern European peoples and especially those of the southeast and also, to some extent, with regard to the other three ancient patriarchates of the East.[5]

7. Since its appearance in world history Christianity, and especially

5. *Das orthodoxe Christentum des Ostens,* Berlin, 1928, p. 23.

Orthodox Chrisitanity, has performed immense service to the Greek people. In the dark years of alien rule the faith preserved by their Church enabled the Greeks to maintain at the same time their language and their national consciousness. We enjoyed from the earliest times a rich monastic and ascetical life which reached its greatest development in the monastic establishment of Mount Athos. This center of Orthodoxy, a bright light set on a mountain, was a focal point of spiritual life and Orthodox culture. As early as the rule of Sultan Mohammed II it had been granted certain specific privileges ($\pi\rho o\nu o\mu\acute{\iota}a$). The chief recipient of these privileges after the Turkish conquest was, however, the ecumenical patriarch of Constantinople. His privileged position had, in fact, already been proclaimed by the Arab caliphs on the basis of the Koran. Under Turkish rule he was acknowledged as the head (Turkish, *milet basi*; Greek, $\dot{\epsilon}\theta\nu\acute{a}\rho\chi\eta s$) of the subject Orthodox peoples and thereby granted a certain autonomy.

The granting of these privileges did not, however, prevent the conquerors from putting an effective stop to any attempt at self-rule and oppressing the subject peoples. The famous church of Hagia Sophia in Constantinople, the churches of Hagia Sophia and Saint Demetrios of Thessalonica, and countless others were turned into mosques. A great number of others were razed to the ground, children were forcibly recruited to serve the Turks, and thousands of Christians (called by the Turks Giours, dogs, slaves) in Epirus, Albania, Bosnia, Serbia, Pontus, Crete, Asia Minor, Cyprus, and other countries were compelled to give up their faith. We know of many martyrs during this period. Even several of the patriarchs—four in the seventeenth century— were hanged.[6] And if the patriarchs, recognized as leaders of their people, were put to death in this terrible way, one can easily imagine the fear and dread which seized the rest of the clergy and their unfortunate people.

The sixteenth century is rightly seen as the darkest age of the Ecumenical Patriarchate and Orthodox Chrisitanity. It was a time of persecution, slavery, and forcible conversion to Islam. Fearful massacres took place in various parts of the immense Ottoman Empire, from Serbia and Rumania to Crete, from Albania and Epirus deep into Asia Minor. This was during the rule of the sultans Selim I (1512–1520), Suleiman II (1520–1560), and Selim II (1566–1574). The last-named called himself "the whip and sword of God," referring, of course, to

6. See Chrysostomos Papadopoulos, *Neomartyrs*, 1934[2] (in Greek).

the task of exterminating the Christian faith. At the end of the six-teenth century Patriarch Meletios Pegas painted a dark picture of this period: "Everywhere where is unrest, terror, sobbing, and crying. No one knows if this evil time will ever come to an end." Despite all this, however, we should remember that it was precisely in this century —about 1590—that Patriarch Jeremias II wrote his famous answers to the letters of the Lutheran theologians of Tübingen.

The situation of the Ecumenical Patriarchate was also very critical in the seventeenth and eighteenth centuries, a time when the sultans recklessly interfered in the internal matters of the Orthodox Churches and compelled Greeks and Serbs to settle in Hungary and Austria.

A compelling witness to the steadfastness of Orthodox Christians in that age of the martyrs are the words of the English historian and diplomat P. Ricaut (1628–1700), who was consul in Smyrna and later vice-regent of Ireland. After visiting several Christian provinces in the East he wrote:

If, as I dare suppose, the divine origins of the Christian religion can be proved by the manner in which different peoples either accept or reject it, the perseverance and steadfastness of the Greeks of today witnesses to its truth. For the steadfastness of the Greek people in the Christian faith can be ascribed only to the special grace of God and his promise that the Gates of Hell would not prevail against the Church.[7]

8. Despite all this there was no lack of missionary effort in the Orthodox Church at that time. Many defended the faith with apostolic zeal and unbelievable heroism. One of these was Kosmas Aetolos, a monk of the monastery of Philotheon on the holy Mount Athos who had studied in the ecclesiastical academy of Athens and repeatedly traversed Thrace, Macedonia, Albania, Epirus, Doris, Parnassis, Aeto-lia, and the islands in the Aegean and Ionian seas. In plain words spoken with the utmost conviction he preached the Gospel, warned Christians of the danger of being torn violently away from the Church, founded more than two hundred schools, and finally died a martyr in Albania. His last words were taken from Psalm 66:12:

We went through fire and through water,
Yet thou hast brought us forth to a spacious place.

Soon after his martyrdom he was recognized by the Greek people as a saint and honored as *Isapostolos* (apostle), though naturally he was

7. P. Ricaut, *Histoire de l'état présent de l'Eglise Grecque et de l'Eglise Arménienne*. 1962, p. 9 ff.

only canonized by the Ecumenical Patriarchate much later (in 1960).

Both Greeks and other Orthodox Christians of the Balkans received their education in the ecclesiastical academy of Mount Athos. Beginning with the eighteenth century, the Ecumenical Patriarchate occupied itself with raising the level of studies and education in general and founded several schools and academies on Mount Athos, in Korfu, Patmos, and Bucharest. Those who taught in these new academies were for the most part clerics who had done their studies in Roman Catholic or Protestant colleges—men like Nikephoros Theotokis, Eugenios Boulgaris, Athanasios Parios, Neophytos Kausokalybites, and others.

At this point we must say something about the part played by the spiritual center called in Greek the *Phanar* with its nobility of high religious and social rank which surrounded the Ecumenical Patriarchate and which even found a place in the Turkish government. Beginning with the eighteenth century, this nobility produced some excellent men, among them high officials and outstanding interpreters. They occupied high posts not only in the Ottoman Empire but also in the principalities of Moldavia and Walachia. They placed a decisive part in raising the cultural level of the Greek people by their work in Christian education and the propagation of Greek humanism. Under the leadership of the Church the organizational reform of the various communities and the raising of their cultural level spread out to the Orthodox faithful of the whole Balkans, especially in the Greek provinces, as also in Asia Minor, the Near East, and the Levantine islands. This implied not only the raising of the cultural level of these peoples but also the beginning of the national rebirth of the Greek people and its partial liberation.

The moving force and main factor in all this cultural activity in Greece as elsewhere in the Orthodox world was *the Church* with its monks, clergy, monasteries, and newly founded schools. The teachers in these schools were, for the most part, clerics who had been educated in the Greek colleges of Constantinople, Athos, Patmos, Bucharest, and Jasi, and even, some of them, in Western Europe.

There began to develop also in the eighteenth century a very active *social movement*. Here as in other activities the Great Church, μεγάλη ἐκκλησία, the Ecumenical Patriarchate, played the leading role. We should stress here in particular the humanistic, educational, and social work of Patriarch Gregory V, who, on Easter Sunday, April 10, 1821, at the beginning of the Greek revolt, was hanged by the Turks to one of the doors of the patriarchal residence.

Already by the middle of the seventeenth century there was considerable scholarly activity in the fields of ancient philology and theology. Greek scholars who had studied in Italy, France, Germany, and Austria left behind a rich deposit of their wisdom.[8] Their activity took in an area which included Russia, Rumania, and Italy. Of these we might mention Meletios Syrigos (†1664); Dositheos, patriarch of Jerusalem (†1707); Meletios, metropolitan of Athens (†1714); Nikodemos Hagiorites (†1809); Eugenios Boulgaris (†1801); Athanasios Parios (†1813) of the Academy of Mount Athos; Nikephoros Theotokis in Rumania; Anthimos Gazis (†1828 in Vienna); Nikolaos Padapoulos Komnenos (†1740 in Italy); and the brothers Lichudae, who had founded a Greco-Slavic academy in Moscow at the beginning of the eighteenth century. Anterior to all these was Maximos Graecos, who as early as the sixteenth century had deserved well of the Russian Church and people. He had come from Arta in Epirus, had studied many years in Italy, and, after a stay on the holy Mount Athos, traveled to Russia and dedicated himself to the service of the Russian sister Church. In this work he suffered persecution for a long time, but after his death in 1556 he was acknowledged and venerated as "the first enlightener of Russia" and later canonized.[9]

9. The Orthodox Church also played a meritorious part in the liberation of its people from alien rule. Even before the actual wars of liberation had broken out, a great contribution had been made by the magnificent Byzantine liturgy, so full of lessons for those who took part in it, as well as by the teachers in the grade schools, who were, for the most part, monks and clerics. In particular, the monasteries were often bulwarks of nationalism.

Monks, bishops, and other clerics took part in the preparations for a national insurrection and even participated in the fighting for freedom. The *Philike Hetaireia* ("Company of Friends"), which first started off the fighting for freedom, had been founded by a group of bishops.

The leader of the first revolt in Rumania, Alexander Hypselantes,

8. An account of this can be found in E. Legrand, *Bibliographie Hellénique*, Vols. VI–XII, K. Sathas, a Greek writer, and others.

9. Gregorias Papamichael, who studied in Russia, has made a lifelong study of this great man, a work published as Μάξιμος ὁ Γραικός, Athens, 1951, 657 pp. It is certainly the most basic study yet to appear on Maximos.

a highly placed Greek officer in the Russian army, had asked for the blessing of the Greek Metropolitan Ignatius of Ungrovlachie in the church of the Three Hierarchs at Iasi before the battle of Dragatsani.[10] On March 25, 1821, Germanos, bishop of Patras, had blessed the colors of the rebel leader in the monastery of Lavra near Kalabryta. At the same time, however, Patriarch Gregory V, whom we named a moment ago,[11] and Adamantios Korais, the well-known physician, ancient philologist, and Hellenist then living in Paris, had grave doubts as to whether the insurrection could succeed. In that year, 1821, several bishops and many clerics and monks died a martyr's death. Among those who fought at Mesolonghi was Joasaph, bishop of Roghi, whose heroic death has been immortalized by Victor Hugo. At this time the history of the Greek Church was indistinguishable from the history of the Greek people. In the fight for liberation the two entered into an inseparable alliance.

10. The Church of Greece only received its autonomy from the Ecumenical Patriarchate twenty years after the founding of the first small, independent Kingdom of Greece in 1850. The Serbs who had risen against Turkish rule as early as 1815 also received their freedom in the Russo-Turkish Treaty of Adrianople in 1829, and at the same time the people of Walachia and Moldavia received their freedom too. The autocephalous Church of Serbia was emancipated from the Ecumenical Patriarchate in 1831 and the Rumanian in 1885. In 1922, after five centuries, the Serbian Patriarchate was reinstituted and recognized by the Ecumenical Patriarchate, and in 1925 there followed the reestablishment and recognition of the Rumanian Patriarchate.

Bulgaria achieved political autonomy only after the Russo-Turkish War of 1876 but remained within the sphere of influence of the Sultan. Already in 1871, however, while still under Turkish rule, the autonomy of the Bulgarian Church was recognized by the Turks, but the Ecumenical Patriarchate hesitated to give way to Russian pressure and recognize an autocephalous Church of Bulgaria, since the people of Bulgaria were as yet not entirely free politically. A year later the Bulgarian Church was declared schismatic by a local council held in Constantinople on account of transgression of the sacred canons of the Orthodox Church, and the heresy of phyletism was condemned.[12]

10. In February, 1821.
11. Martyred in 1821.
12. Phyletism, rather like Gallicanism, is a preponderance of political influence in Church matters. See Ch. Papadopoulos, *Die Kirche Bulgariens*, 1957.

In 1945 the Bulgarian schism was ended by the Ecumenical Patriarchate, and the independence of the Bulgarian Church recognized. In 1962 Bulgaria became an independent patriarchate.[13]

11. In spite of the Bulgarian schism the Orthodox nations of the Balkans—Greece, Serbia, and Bulgaria—came together in 1912 in a political alliance in the name of the Christian Orthodox faith. In the same year they declared war on the Turks with the purpose of freeing other Orthodox peoples from subjection. The first Balkan war, and the second which followed soon afterwards, achieved the important result that various elements among the population of Greece, Serbia, Bulgaria, and Rumania could be reunited with their own national state and their own autocephalous Church. The metropolitans of the new Greek provinces were, however, obliged to retain the name of the ecumenical patriarch in their liturgy. The partially autonomous Churches of Crete and the Dodecanese remained, however, under the jurisdiction of the Ecumenical Patriarchate according to ecclesiastical law.

Even before the outbreak of the Russian Revolution of 1917 the Russian Church had reestablished the ancient patriarchate of Moscow. Patriarch Tychon was recognized by the Ecumenical Patriarchate. I cannot deal here in detail with the difficulties experienced by the Russian Church at that time in the matter of ecclesiastical law and in other respects. I limit myself to noting that new Orthodox Churches arose at this time in Georgia, Poland, Estonia, Latvia, Lithuania, Finland, and Czechoslovakia. All of these were recognized by the other Orthodox Churches.

As a result of the Balkan wars, both World Wars, and especially the catastrophe which took place in Asia Minor in 1922, the territory of the Ecumenical Patriarchate has been reduced to a minimum; in fact, it consists almost exclusively of the region of Constantinople (Istanbul). But the spiritual, historical, and canonical significance of the Ecumenical Patriarchate, the primacy of its patriarch as *primus inter pares* among the other Orthodox Church leaders, its renown in the whole Christian world, remain undiminished. The Pan-Orthodox conferences at Rhodes, in 1961, 1963, and 1964, and the celebrations to mark the thousandth anniversary of Mount Athos in 1963, demonstrated very clearly both the unity of the Orthodox Church and the strength of the primacy of the ecumenical patriarch in Orthodoxy.

All the ancient patriarchates were for centuries occupied by Greeks.

13. G. Konidaris, *The Removal of the Bulgarian Schism,* 1958 (in Greek).

This was true of the Patriarchate of *Antioch,* the third in order of importance, until 1899, when a Pan-Arabic movement in that region supported by the Pan-Slav movement, succeeded in transferring it to Arabs. The Patriarchate of *Jerusalem* remained Greek, as did that of *Alexandria,* though the latter was strongly challenged by the Pan-Arabic movement which had made great headway in Egypt. Without the Greek element, however, the new possibilities which are opening in Africa to the Patriarchate of Alexandria will not be so easily grasped.

Still remaining under the jurisdiction of the Ecumenical Patriarchate are the federation of monasteries on Mount Athos, the Greek-Orthodox churches in West Europe, and those in the United States, Canada, South America, and New Zealand.

THE FOUNDATIONS
OF ORTHODOX
BELIEF

MY PURPOSE here is not to give a general review of Orthodox faith, a faith which in many respects has not yet been perfectly developed and worked out, but simply to throw some light on the basic character- istics of this faith and to bring out those points in particular which distinguish the Orthodox Church from the other great Churches. I hope that this small volume will not be taken to be a polemical or apologetic tract. Such an outcome would be against its purpose, and, in any case, there is no more room for such an approach in this age when everyone is seeking for greater mutual understanding.

THE SOURCES

In the first place we have to tackle the question of the sources of the teaching of the Orthodox Church and how she stands with regard to divine revelation.[1] In this fundamental question there are consid- erable differences between the Churches.

Both in Orthodoxy and the Roman Catholic Church the sources of Christian doctrine are the Bible and Tradition. Together they form the treasure-house of supernatural revelation. The Church dispenses this treasure: she is the authentic witness and interpreter of Scripture and tradition. The Bible is the written record of apostolic tradition which was put in writing on specific occasions and for specific purposes. Church, Bible, and tradition constitute for Orthodoxy an indivisible unity. Neither the Bible nor tradition renders the other expendable. On the contrary, they are mutually complementary and explanative. The Bible must be interpreted and completed in the light of apostolic tradition and read within the Church.

As the custodian of the Scriptures the Church has the assistance of

---

1. See P. Bratsiotis, *Die Autorität der Bibel heute*, Zürich, 1951, pp. 19–33; B. Vellas, "Die Heilige Schrift in der Griechisch-Orthodoxen Kirche," in *Die Orthodoxe Kirche in griechischer Sicht*, I, pp. 121–140.

the Holy Spirit sent to her by Christ to lead her into all truth (John
16:13). The Bible has a special place in the Orthodox Church since it
is the touchstone of faith and the means of mediating tradition. We
take the view, however, that its validity derives from the Church,
which is "the pillar and bulwark of the truth" (I Tim 3:15). With
the Bible the Church is established on the firmest basis, which is the
living God.

According to the Orthodox view, sacred tradition contains nothing
which contradicts the Scriptures and overlaps to a considerable extent
with them. Both are the work of one and the same divine Spirit dwelling in the Church. In the Orthodox Church both have the same importance and validity since, as St. Basil says, "if we attempt to put aside
the unwritten words [of tradition] as if they had no great value, without knowing it we do considerable hurt to the Gospel."[2] We are speaking here, however, in the first place of the apostolic tradition which
was passed on from mouth to mouth and from generation to generation, yet which remained essentially unaltered, in the undivided
Church of the first eight centuries. The Orthodox Church, which sees
itself as the true and direct descendant of the ancient Catholic Church,
recognizes neither the so-called branch theory, according to which
each individual Church possesses a part of ancient tradition nor
one authoritative teaching authority residing in one single ecclesiastical office. The Church *in her entire fullness* (ὅλον τὸ πλήρωμα)
is the bearer of the true apostolic tradition and the guardian of
orthodoxy, a truth strikingly paraphrased by the Orthodox patriarchs
in 1848: "The 'body of the Church,' that is, the People of God itself,
is the guardian of the true faith."

The Church regards as her voice the *hierarchy* which comes together
in ecumenical councils. The ecumenical character of these councils
and the infallibility of their decisions are guaranteed by the fact that
they are accepted at least tacitly by the entire body of the Church,
clergy *and* laity, since the Holy Spirit can only be said to dwell in the
Church as a whole (see John 15:26 and 16:23). On this basis our
Church understands tradition as something not static (as some theologians of other confessions suppose) but dynamic. On the other hand,
however, we do not believe that this dynamic power can take tradition
away from its origins. In the last analysis the apostolic tradition is
understood by the Orthodox Church as a treasure which she keeps in
the consciousness of faith and which remains always living since the

2. *De sancto spiritu*, XXIX.

divine Spirit dwells in the Church. By its very nature the tradition remains unchanged; it can, however, be further explained, developed, and deepened.

In addition to the supernatural revelation of God, which is what the Scriptures are mainly about and which constitutes revelation properly so called, orthodox together with Roman Catholic theology recognizes an indirect or *natural revelation.*

This kind of revelation is not only attested in holy Scripture (Rom 1:19 and 2:14) but is also, in some way, contained in holy Scripture. Natural revelation does not exclude supernatural but rather requires it, and the latter presupposes the former. Natural revelation, which is the object of "natural theology," has its justification, on the one hand, in the external cosmos and human conscience and, on the other, in world history. It is not, however, sufficient in itself, but must be completed by supernatural revelation (see Rom 1:19 and 2:14; 1 Cor 1:21). It is imperfect in that it is involved with the human spirit, which chiefly because of sin, cannot fully comprehend revelation. We can best describe the Orthodox attitude to natural revelation by quoting a remark of Origen: "Human nature is incapable of itself of seeking God and finding him securely without his help. He can be found only by the man who admits that he needs him and he reveals himself only to those to whom he will."[3]

Following the Greek Fathers of the Church, Orthodox theology accepts not only natural revelation but also a *natural knowledge of God,* which, however, is always insufficient of itself, imperfect and subject to perversion. There is, in fact, always something ambiguous about natural revelation, with the result that often, instead of leading men to God, it impels them to make false gods for themselves.

We conclude then that the acceptance of natural revelation by sinful and imperfect men has always been imperfect and will remain so, being often misunderstood and in such a way that supernatural revelation is necessary for the salvation of men. We must add, however, that supernatural revelation, as it comes to us in this present world, has its limits and must be perfected at the end of time in the life of the world to come, when "his servants . . . shall see his face. . . . And night shall be no more; they need no light of lamp or sun, for the Lord God will be their light" (Rev 22:4–5). In the meantime, even the perfect revelation of God in Christ remains to some extent dim and darkened in those to whom it is addressed, and can only be grasped by faith and

3. *Contra Celsum,* VII, 42.

by divine grace cooperating freely with the natural spiritual forces of man. "For now we see in a mirror dimly, but then face to face" (1 Cor 13:12), or, with Ambrose, "Umbra in lege, imago in evangelio, veritas in coelestibus."[4]

With regard to *the unity of the Bible* and its authority seen from the Orthodox point of view, we should note the following: although the Bible consists of many different books written by different authors at different times, and is divided into two parts belonging to two different worlds, the multiplicity of writings are gathered together in one book which forms one organic unity. Full of diversity as it is, it is inspired from beginning to end by the one divine Spirit, deals with the same theme throughout, and has for its center the one reality of Christ. It begins with the creation of heaven and earth and ends with the appearance of the "new heavens and new earth." For Orthodox theology, however, this unity of the Bible does not imply an equality of Old Testament revelation with that contained in the New. The New Testament takes in much more than the Old and is superior to it. The relation existing between them is that of preparation, presupposition, prophecy, and type on the one hand and fulfillment on the other.

With regard to *the structure of the Scriptures,* we should note that Orthodox theology rejects verbal inspiration understood in the literal sense. On the one hand, the Bible is for us a communication of divine truths; on the other, the Holy Spirit watches over the way in which these truths are expressed, but always in view of the peculiar character of each of the inspired writers. As in its doctrine of the Word of God made flesh, so here, in its theology of holy Scripture as the written Word of God, Orthodox theology distinguishes between a divine and a human element and takes the Bible to be *divine* in its essence but *human* in the form in which it comes to us. *Inspiration* has to do above all with the essence of what the Bible says, although it often affects the form in which the truths of salvation are expressed, even though we regard this latter as the area in which the human initiative of the inspired author has free play. In the words of Augustine, "in scripturis per hominem, more hominum, loquitur Deus."[5]

Orthodox theology distinguishes between different degrees of scriptural inspiration, and among these that of the prophets (understood in the broadest sense) and the Apostles is the highest. This is expressed

4. "Under the law the shadow, in the Gospel the image, in heaven the truth itself."
5. "God speaks in the Scriptures through men, in the way that men speak."

fully and appositely by the Apostle Paul: "There is one glory of the sun, and another glory of the moon, and another glory of the stars; for star differs from star in glory" (1 Cor 15:41). Corresponding to the inspiration of Scripture is its power to work within us. This power is the outcome of the spiritual grace (πνευματικὴ χάρις) which resides in it. This is how the Church Fathers spoke of it,[6] and the Protestant theologians of the seventh century referred to it as the "testimonium Spiritus Sancti." Although these Fathers recognized a sanctifying power in the Scriptures, which they regard as the fruit of individual Bible reading stemming ultimately from the spiritual grace to which we referred a moment ago, they did not regard this bestowal of grace as the basic criterion for judging the authority of the Scriptures, and in this the Orthodox Church follows them.

With regard to the question of *the authority of the Scriptures in matters of faith and morals*—one which is rather too much to the fore in theological circles today—we should make the following comment from the Orthodox point of view. Sacred Scripture, like divine revelation in general, has for its aim the salvation of men. It is self-evident, therefore, that the authority of Scripture refers especially to anything in it dealing with the salvation of men. But in the Orthodox Church salvation is not considered as coming exclusively either from faith or from grace (*sola fide* or *sola gratia*). It is rather the result of a cooperation of divine grace with human freedom, or, put in another way, the outcome of faith which works through and is expressed in love (see Gal 5:6). The question at issue is always salvation, and this is not merely tied to particular events in the course of the history of salvation or to particular truths of faith connected with these, but also to ethical principles and commandments, especially those which relate to the revelation of God in Christ and prescribe a way of living commensurate with faith: "All Scripture is inspired by God and profitable for teaching, for reproof, for correction, and for training in righteousness" (2 Tim 3:16). This means, not that the Bible is a handbook of ethical instruction, but that it offers us moral principles and divine commandments, compliance with which in faith is indispensable for salvation.[7]

In questions of faith and morals Orthodox theology clearly gives the predominant role to the New Testament. The Old Testament is not left aside on account of the imperfection which it contains nor

6. See Theodoret in Migne, P. G., 82, 676; Amphilochios in P. G., 37, 597.
7. See Matt 7:21 ff; Rev 14:13; 20:13; 22:14.

is it used for its own sake on account of its witness to divine revelation; it is used only in association with the New Testament and in the light of the New Testament. The New Testament is the fulfillment of the Old. It is the midpoint in the light of which the Old must be evaluated and the criterion according to which we have to study it (see Matt 5:17–18). The consequence of this for Orthodox theological thinking is that we may seek instruction in the Old Testament and its development in questions of faith and morals, but we would not simply quote Old Testament texts apropos the questions that preoccupy us today without also quoting parallel New Testament texts. We use only a Christocentric approach to Scripture interpretation. An indiscriminate use of Old and New Testament texts in matters of faith and morals will inevitably lead to an obscuring of the true spirit of the Christian life, and this has happened repeatedly in the history of theology and of the Church.

The moral content of the Scriptures has a dual origin. It is at the same time partly the result of natural revelation, by reason of the law of conscience which is implanted in the human heart, and partly the outcome of supernatural revelation. The moral law which springs from natural revelation is confirmed and corrected in the light of that supernatural revelation with which the natural revelation contained in the Bible is closely interwoven. We find two forms of moral instruction in the Scriptures: on the one hand, laws and regulations; on the other, general principles or commands related to moral character, the motivation of human activity, or ethics in general.

This last element, met with very often in the Old Testament and even found in the Law of Moses, is the predominant and characteristic note of New Testament religion, which is to the highest degree ethical by nature. In opposition to it stands the legalism which to a great extent characterizes Old Testament ethics. The Old Testament morality of law-observance is superseded by the ethic of the Gospel by reason of that spirit of freedom and grace which is specific to it.

A third distinction has to be made between different parts of the Scriptures which have a moral content. Many stipulations of the Law of Moses and many of the moral admonitions of the Old Testament have a merely fortuitous and transitory character, whereas the religious and ethical principles of the New Testament have permanent validity. This at least is the view generally taken by Christians, and certainly by Greek Orthodox Christians.

At the same time the opposition between Law and Gospel is not exaggerated in Orthodox theology, despite the admitted insufficiency of the Law to achieve human salvation and the superiority of the Gospel over the Law in so many respects. The Law, in fact, is seen as having the character of "a custodian until Christ came" (Gal 3:24). The use of the formula "law of the Gospel" which occurs in some Fathers of the Church and is also retained by some Protestant theologians to designate the ethical demands of Christ seems to us justified.[8] We are of the opinion that such a view can be adequately supported from the New Testament itself. In the first place, the concept of "law" is closely associated with "the Kingdom of God," which in its turn is not so far away from the idea of *theocracy, divine rule,* understood in the widest sense of the term; not far enough away, certainly, to justify the fears entertained by many theologians in this regard. Even the concept of "covenant" is not alien to the idea of law, since both express in different ways *the will of God.*

At this point there arises the question of the antithesis expressed by Jesus in the Sermon on the Mount between the commandments which he gives and those of the Law of Moses. I am referring here to the so-called antitheses: "you have heard that it was said of old . . . but I say to you" (Matt 5:21 ff). But the whole context of the Sermon on the Mount conveys the impression that from now on a new law takes the place of the old:[9] Jesus goes up "on the mountain" and there instructs his disciples; there is here a clearly conscious parallelism with Sinai, and in fact the whole presentation of the Sermon in Matthew leads us to read it as the *Magna Carta* of the Kingdom of God understood as the entire community, not just the circle of the apostles. In the Fourth Gospel, too, we find reference to the commandments (ἐντολαί) of Christ.[10]

This evangelical law has about it the character of "good news" (gospel). It is described and paraphrased as: "the law of the Spirit of life in Christ Jesus" (Rom 8:2), "the law of Christ" (Gal 6:2), "the perfect law of liberty" (James 2:8). It is summed up and brought to fulfillment in the double law of love of God and the neighbor (Matt 22:40; Rom 13:10) and is inseparably linked with the practice of the Christian virtues without thereby losing its unique characteristics in a haphazard multiplicity of other elements of New Testament teaching.

8. See, for example, C. H. Dodd, *Gospel and Law,* Cambridge, 1957[2].

9. See, for example, the end of the Sermon on the Mount, Matt 7:24; also Matt 28:20 and Luke 17:10.

10. John 13:34; 14:15, 21; 15:10, 12; 1 John 5:3; John 5 ff.

The moral law of the Decalogue is not abrogated by the Gospel. It is still in force as a divine law throughout the whole Christian world and is to be seen as a preparatory step toward the Gospel in which it is fulfilled. For this reason the Ten Commandments, together with the Sermon on the Mount, form part of the Orthodox Church's catechism. To sum up, Orthodox theology sees New Testament moral teaching as the fulfillment and perfection not only of the Law and the moral teaching of the Old Testament in general but also of the natural moral law.

As regards *the relation between the moral message of the Bible and political and social ethics,* the view of Orthodox theologians can be stated more or less as follows. We have to admit, first of all, that the Bible does not contain specific laws governing civil life, social behavior, and political relations either of individuals or of nations. Likewise, it cannot be doubted that, in part, bibilical morality—especially that contained in the Old Testament—is provisional and transitory. At the same time, however, Orthodox theology believes that the Scriptures contain a definite ethic of permanent validity and that this ethic, taken with faith in Christ, must inspire and regulate the attitudes of the Church and of each individual Christian in political and social questions for as long as the Church remains in this world, "so that you may prove what is the will of God, what is good and acceptable and perfect" (Rom 12:2). The essence of this scriptural ethic is made up of reverence for the human person, social righteousness, and love for others even to the sacrifice of one's own life.

Taken all in all, Orthodox theology does not accept the idea that it is justifiable to apply specific stipulations found in the Bible to the social or political conditions of modern times, much less just to take over institutions such as the sabbatical year or the year of jubilees. Nor does it seek in the Bible specific indications or programs for political or social life or even for the direction of the personal life of the individual believer. At the same time, however, the Orthodox Church strongly holds that we can find a spirit and moral approach not limited to a specific place and time in the institutions and moral and religious principles of the Old Testament, even more so in "the law of the Gospel" and the example of New Testament saints, in the first place the Redeemer himself. We can and must bring this spirit to bear on the spiritual life of the individual believer and of Christian communities in such a way that it is really put into practice. This must go together with that biblical ethic, especially as contained in the New

Testament, which we said possesses permanent validity. In this way the Church of our time, with those who truly belong to it, can take up that spirit of fellowship and community which was the motive force behind such Old Testament religious and social institutions as the Sabbath, sabbatical year, year of jubilees, and such. The Church will also be reminded of the limits set on the rights of the individual in the Old and New Testaments, including the right to private property. It will not overlook the prudent attitude of Jesus and the Apostles to the Roman Empire and its institutions,[11] or even the attempt of the early Church to realize the ideal of the common life based on love. Even less will it feel entitled to part company with the social ideal of the Old and New Testaments as seen, for example, in the Deuteronomic injunction "there shall be no poor among you" (Deut 15:4) put into practice by the early Church: "there was not a needy person among them" (Acts 4:34).

A "double-standard ethic" (that is, one standard for Christians, one for non-Christians) has no place in Orthodox theology since it is unknown both to the New Testament and the Fathers of the Church. Orthodox theologians recognize that the Bible contributes to the discovery and elucidation of the natural law. The existence of such a law can be documented from the very earliest period of history among diverse peoples of the earth in the form of different social institutions such as the family, community, and nation. We also find it expressed in the form of aphorisms such as the Golden Rule formulated either positively or negatively.[12] The existence of the natural law is evidently presupposed in many of the laws and stipulations of the Old Testament and is recognized quite explicitly in the New Testament (see Rom 2:14; 13:1). At the same time, however, what we said earlier about natural religion also applies here. The innate natural moral law (or moral law of nature) which is written on the heart does not render the supernatural law, the law of grace, superfluous. On the contrary, this latter presupposes the natural law and makes up for its deficiencies. It cannot be compared with it, as if both were on the same level; this confusion between natural law and Christian ethics has in practice proved disastrous, and as long as Christian morality, no matter in what theological terms it finds expression, wishes to lay serious claim to

11. See, for example, Matt 18:27; 22:2; Rom 13:1 ff; 1 Tim 2:2; Philem.
12. See Tob 4:15, "Do not do to others what you would not wish them to do to you," and the Golden Rule in Matt 6:12, "Whatever you wish that men would do to you, do so to them."

being Christian, it must remain distinct and unadulterated. We should state in conclusion that a theology of natural law has yet to be elaborated by Orthodox theology.

THE MEANING OF DOGMA

One fundamental difference between the major Churches is the way in which they conceive of dogma.[13] As we see it, Protestantism is characterized, on the one hand, by an overemphasis on the human element in dogma—and, correspondingly, a rather loose definition of its mandatory character—and, on the other, by a fear of dogma in general. Roman Catholic teaching comes fairly near to the Orthodox position insofar as it accepts not only dogmas solemnly defined by the Church but also those which feature in its ordinary teaching. Like the Orthodox Church, it holds to their mandatory character. The Orthodox view differs from that of the Roman Catholic Church in the following respects:

1. Whereas in the Roman Catholic Church the pope is able, since the First Vatican Council, to state what is to be believed "ex sese, non ex consensu ecclesiae,"[14] the Orthodox Church holds that only ecumenical councils have the right of officially proclaiming dogmas, since they share in the common conviction of the Orthodox Church and express its *sensus communis*.

2. Orthodoxy seeks the bases of dogma in both Scripture and tradition, but this tradition must be well attested from ancient times in accordance with the classical definition of Vincent of Lerins: "quod ubique, quod semper, quod ab omnibus creditum est."

3. In keeping with what is sometimes referred to as the devout agnosticism of the Greek Church Fathers who stress the element of mystery in the divine truths, the Orthodox Church strives to avoid the abuse of logical categories in formulating dogmas.

As regards the way dogma is viewed in Orthodox theology, we should say that there are two main ways of looking at it: one, the best represented, which is conservative; the other, which comes closer to the Protestant position. According to this latter, which is really only

13. Grandmaison, *Le dogme chrétien*, 1928; B. Bartmann, *Lehrbuch der Dogmatik*, I, 1928; E. Brunner, *Dogmatik*, I, pp. 111–113; P. Bratsiotis, "La signification du dogme dans la Théologie orthodoxe," in *L'Eglise et les églises*, Ed. de Chèvetogne. II, 1954, pp. 197–206.
14. Denzinger, *Enchiridion*, par. 1792, 1839.

widespread among Slavic theologians, chiefly under the influence of Stephen Zankow, and which is unfortunately thought by Western theologians to be the predominant view in the Orthodox Church in general,[15] dogma is really quite peripheral. According to Zankow, Orthodox Church dogma can be reduced to the Trinity and the Incarnation as expounded by the ecumenical councils. Dogma is genuine doctrine proposed by an ecumenical council and accepted by the whole Church, and only a proposition laid down in this way can have the mandatory force of dogma; we have to make a clear distinction between dogmas, theologoumena, and what is merely a question of theological opinion.[16]

This liberal view, which finds no firm support either in primitive theology or in that of the Byzantine Church, has been rejected almost unanimously by Greek theologians who follow ancient theological tradition. The reasons are as follows:

1. In the writings of the Fathers of the Church we never find the idea that only those doctrines have binding force which have been formulated by an ecumenical council and recognized by the Church. According to them, on the contrary, every proposition of faith is binding which is preserved in the consciousness of the Church as a whole, quite apart from the question whether it has been officially formulated and proclaimed by an ecumenical council.

2. This limitation of the meaning of dogma presupposes that the Church had no dogma during the first three centuries of its existence. This is not so.

3. The ecumenical councils have, in the first place, elevated those Christian truths to dogmas which were either disputed or misunderstood by heretics. If it were true that only propositions emanating from ecumenical councils could have the status of dogma, we should have to draw the conclusion that these latter owed their origin to purely extrinsic and fortuitous circumstances. This is clearly false. We should also have to conclude that such basic truths of faith as the canon of holy Scripture, the doctrine of the Church, biblical inspiration, grace, justification, the sacraments, and the like have no binding character. They would be mere theologoumena or even a matter of theological opinion and nothing more, and would thereby be in constant jeopardy.

4. Last but not least, if this were so there would have been no rea-

15. See F. Heiler, *Urkirche und Ostkirche*, pp. 188 f; E. Brunner, *op. cit.*, I, p. 112.
16. S. Zankow, *Orthodoxes Christentum des Ostens*, Berlin, 1928, pp. 37 ff.

son at all for the division of the Church, and its unity could be simply reestablished on the basis of the creed of Nicaea-Constantinople.

Because of all these very weighty reasons, alluded to by Professor Demetrius Balanos, by no means a conservative thinker, modern Greek dogmatic theologians such as Rossis, Androutsos, Dyoboyniotis, Karmiris, and Trembelas recognize as dogmas "all those theoretical truths of faith which are taught by sacred Scripture and tradition and which have been proposed by the Church for the acceptance of the faithful from the earliest times."[17] Worth noting, finally, in this connection is the distinction between East and West appropriately referred to by Emil Brunner in his *Dogmatik,* a distinction consisting in the fact that "there [that is, in the East] the dogmatic element predominates, while here [in the West] it is more the juridical."[18]

THE KNOWLEDGE OF GOD

With regard to the knowledge of God,[19] a theme of equal importance to the one we have just been discussing, we should say that what is emphasized in the Orthodox Church is the nature of God as being beyond the experience and powers of expression of natural man. This is in keeping with what we find in Scripture and the teaching of the Church Fathers, especially those writing in Greek, from Justin, Clement of Alexandria, and Origen down to the Cappadocians, Cyril of Jerusalem, John Chrysostom, and John Damascene. On this point Gregory of Nazianzen remarks: "What alone we can understand of him [that is, God] is that he can be neither experienced nor understood."[20] Cyril of Jerusalem states: "to admit that we do not know is to know much . . . in things concerning God." John Chrysostom says, in a phrase which has much influenced Rudolph Otto, "there is one true knowledge, and that is not to know," an expression which is reminiscent of the famous dictum of Socrates: ἓν οἶδα ὅτι οὐδὲν οἶδα ("I know one thing, that I know nothing").[21] This approach explains the special prominence of so-called apophatic and mystical theology

17. D. Balanos, *Einleitung in die Dogmengeschichte,* 1919, pp. 10 f.
18. E. Brunner, *op. cit.,* I, p. 111.
19. See J. Karmiris, *op. cit.,* p. 29; P. Evdokimov, *L'Orthodoxie,* 1960, pp. 174–176.
20. *Hom.,* 45, 3; cf. John Damascene, *Expos. fidei orthodoxae,* I, 8.
21. J. Daniélou, *Introduction aux Homélies de St. Jean Chrysostome sur l'incompréhension de Dieu,* Sources Chrétiennes, Vol. 28, 1951; H. de Lubac, *Sur les chemins de Dieu,* 1956; R. Otto, *The Idea of the Holy,* 1935; John Meyendorf, *Die Orthodoxe Kirche,* 1961, pp. 213 ff.

in the Orthodox Church. We have to remember, however, that for Orthodoxy knowledge of God comes not merely through faith but also by learning to recognize what God has done. In this way the Orthodox Church avoids two extremes, one ancient and the other modern: on the one hand, the "perfect knowledge of God" of the Gnostics and Eunomians; on the other, agnosticism whether of classical or more recent stamp. We should note, finally, the role of mysticism in the Orthodox Church, of special importance for the doctrine of the atonement, for an understanding of the Christian doctrines of Incarnation and Redemption—as far as it is possible to understand them—and for the doctrine of God in general.

The Holy Spirit

The doctrine of the Holy Spirit and his gift of grace is of extraordinary significance in the Orthodox Church. The Holy Spirit is the chief factor in the establishment of the Church, by giving us divine graces for our own use, sanctifying and divinizing us, helping us to administer the sacraments rightly, leading the Church to attain her end and find the truth in accordance with the promise of the Lord (John 15:26; cf. 14:26). For this reason we sing on the vigil of Pentecost: "The Holy Spirit is the giver of all; he raises up prophecy, perfects the priests, gives wisdom to the ignorant, and makes fishermen into men learned in divine things. It is he who makes the whole Church one." And again: "Heavenly King, consoler, Spirit of truth, all-present and all-fulfilling, treasure of good things and giver of life, come, take up your dwelling in us, purify us from every stain, and save, O Merciful One, our souls."

The Holy Spirit is the soul of the Church. He is the comforter and the representative of Christ. It is through him that the work of salvation is completed and the faithful are sanctified. It will be clear from this that the Orthodox Church remains emphatically at one with the traditional belief in the divinity of the Holy Spirit and his procession from the Father. Zankow remarks pertinently that "the great struggle about the *Filioque* clause was not just a battle of words."[22] Indicative of the significance of the Holy Spirit in the totality of Orthodox belief are the quotations given above from the liturgy of the vigil of Pentecost, the sublime "Orthros" and the celebration of the Great Vespers with the splendid hymns to the Holy Spirit and the seven

22. S. Zankow, *op. cit.*, p. 44.

deeply moving prayers recited by the kneeling priest while all the congregation also remains kneeling. In them we praise the marvelous outpouring of the Holy Spirit and, at the same time, the exceeding mystery of "the Three in One, alike in nature and indivisible, though distinguished, one from the other."[23] Without any exaggeration we can characterize the Orthodox Church as "pneumatic," filled with the divine Spirit (*Pneuma*).

THE INCARNATION OF THE WORD AND THE DIVINIZATION OF MAN

Following the teaching of the New Testament and the ancient Church, the dogma of the Incarnation of the Word has a unique and central importance for the Orthodox Church. Linked with this is the doctrine of the divinization (*theosis*) of man: "Factus est quod sumus nos, ut nos perficeret esse quod est ipse."[24] This is the celebrated phrase enunciated by Irenaeus, Bishop of Lyons, who came from Asia Minor. It was repeated in other words by Clement of Alexandria a little later and then taken up in terms which were practically identical by Athanasius: "He became man so that we might become divine."[25] At a later date Gregory of Nyssa and Cyril of Alexandria set out this theology in a more systematic form. Taken all in all, this teaching on *theosis*, which is the center of Christology and, so to speak, the obverse of the doctrine of the Incarnation, is at the same time the axis of the Christian doctrine of redemption and a special characteristic of the Orthodox Church and its theology. This teaching on the divinization of man, which, as Heiler pertinently remarks, was an essential structural element in early Christian thought, does not of course imply that man is no longer a creature. Rather, human nature is united with the divine nature, penetrated by it, and transformed as iron is in fire.[26]

Intimately connected with this central doctrine of the Eastern Church is the predominant place given to the Virgin Mother of the God-Man Jesus Christ. This is in keeping with the honor in which she

23. It should be noted that the great Pentecost liturgy is celebrated at the ordination of a bishop in the Orthodox Church.

24. Irenaeus, *Adversus Haereses*, V, in P. G., 7, 1120.

25. *De Incarnatione*, 2, 54, in P. G., 25, 192; cf. *Contra Arianos*, I, 38, 39; II, 47, 70; III, 34.

26. F. Heiler, *op. cit.*, pp. 211, 557; Lot-Borodine, "La doctrine de la déification dans l'Église Grecque," *Revue de l'Histoire des Religions*, 1932–1933; A. Theodorou, *The Teaching of the Orthodox Church on Theosis*, Athens, 1956 (in Greek); P. Bratsiotis, "Die Theosislehre der Orthodoxen Kirche," in *Mededelingen van de Koninklijke Vlaamse Akademie*, Klasse der Letteren, 1961, Nr. 1.

was held in the early Church and in the entire Church before the schism, as it can be seen in the second and third ecumenical councils. She was honored both as perpetual virgin (ἀειπάρθενος) and, in the time-honored phrase first used by Origen, the God-bearer (θεοτόκος).

THE NATURE OF MAN

Since the doctrine of the Incarnation is so intimately connected with the Christian view of man and his nature—to the extent that this doctrine presupposes the latter—I think it would be expedient here to give a brief sketch of how our Church understands man and his nature. I will concentrate especially on those points on which we differ from the other major Christian bodies and leave aside the doctrine common to all about the First Man and his state of perfection before the Fall.

According to Orthodox teaching, man before the Fall was endowed by God with extraordinary spiritual and moral gifts, for which reason the Scripture says that he was made in the image of God. With the help of divine grace and by making use of the gifts given to him, which together formed the so-called *iustitia originalis* (the original state of justice), he was to become like (καθ' ὁμοίωσιν) to God. The lapse into sin is therefore a separation between the first man and God, though this does not at all imply a complete estrangement of man from his Creator; it brings with it a darkening of the intellect, not a complete destruction of the image of God in man. This obscuring of the image of God brought with it a weakening and distortion of the spiritual and moral nature of man, a proneness to evil and a deliverance to the death of the body. At the same time, however, there remained the ability not only to seek after God but to do good (see Rom 2:14 f).

The position of our Church with regard to natural theology and the law of nature is to be understood on the basis of this doctrine of primitive state of man and the consequences of the Fall. We do not, however, exclude the Mother of God from these consequences of original sin and therefore, despite our great veneration for Mary, cannot accept the Roman Catholic dogma of the Immaculate Conception.

THE WORK OF REDEMPTION
AND ITS APPROPRIATION

With regard to the redemptive power of the death of Jesus on the cross, we should say first of all that for the Orthodox Church, at least for the Greek Orthodox Church, the whole redemptive work of Jesus Christ which culminated on the cross remains a deep mystery which human understanding is not capable of penetrating. This means that Greek Orthodoxy is very slow to accept certain attempts, current in the West, to explain this mystery. It is content with the general statement that the redemptive power of the death of Jesus makes complete atonement to the divine justice and avoids speaking of a superabundance of merits of the death on the cross, a "treasury of the merits of Christ and the saints," and the like. Instead of speculating on the redemptive significance of the death of Christ, the Orthodox Church prefers to emphasize the Resurrection, which it sees as the culmination, the triumphant conclusion, of Christ's redemptive activity and which it grasps in faith as the pledge of the final victorious outcome of salvation, of eternal life and transfiguration. This explains the extraordinary significance of the feast of Easter in Orthodox liturgy.

As for *the appropriation of redemption and salvation,* we can say that it comes about through the grace of the Holy Spirit, the cooperation of our free effort "in fear and trembling," and, consequently, the spiritual strengthening of the Christian with the help of the grace that comes to him through the redemptive activity of Christ. Out position here is far removed from either the Pelagian or the Augustinian view. Indicative of Orthodox teaching is the remark of Cyril of Jerusalem: "It is for God to give, for you to receive and preserve."[27] In his sixteenth homily on the Epistle to the Romans John Chrysostom says:

It does not merely depend on whether a person wills it himself or no, but on God, whether he shows mercy or no. He does not take away the ability to will it, but he shows him that not everything depends on himself, but that rather he needs grace from on high. Then a person can make the act of will and go forward to salvation, not, however, trusting in his own efforts but rather in the mercy of God.

For our Church the culmination, the greatest gift that follows on redemption, is the *theosis,* or divinization, of which we have spoken earlier. This is the ultimate purpose of the creation of man. But of course this has to be interpreted in a spiritual and moral sense, not at all as a mechanical or magical process as Ritschl and Adolf Harnack supposed.[28]

27. *Catechesis,* I, 4.
28. See E. Brunner, *Der Mittler,* pp. 219–233.

ECCLESIOLOGY

The doctrine of the Church is the most difficult and probably the most complicated of all the dogmatic questions which separate the individual Christian confessions. In the Church the Incarnation is continued and the work of redemption is carried on, but she is at the same time, in the metaphor of the Apostle Paul, "the body of Christ whose head he is" (Rom 12:4–5; 1 Cor 12:12 ff; Eph 1:22 ff; Col 1:18, 24). The work of redemption begun and completed by Christ is continued in the Church, but the precise manner in which redemption in Christ is appropriated leads to a major difference in opinions between the Churches. This is one of the main reasons why all the various divergencies of view in the individual Churches tend to concentrate on the doctrine of the nature of the Church. On the basis of Scripture and tradition we Orthodox distinguish not only between the Church militant and triumphant but also between the visible and invisible parts of the one Church. As for the nature of the Church, the Orthodox Catholic, together with the Roman Catholic, cherishes a common inheritance from the undivided ancient Church. He sees the Church as a divine-human organism, the mystical Body of Christ, as an institution founded by God having both a visible reality (the body) and an invisible reality (the soul of the Church). This is in opposition to the Protestant view, according to which the essence of the Church lies in its invisible nature, the *communio sanctorum,* a fellowship of saints outwardly unknown to each other who have no need of a priesthood instituted by God for their government and sanctification. To state it more exactly, the Orthodox Church does not overemphasize either the invisible or the visible element, but tries to maintain a balance between the two.

Leaving aside many individual points of disagreement, Orthodoxy is at one with the Roman Catholic Church and opposed to Protestantism in viewing the Church as infallible insofar as she is led by the spirit of God which dwells in her according to Christ's promise (John 14:6; 16:3). It is for this reason that Paul describes her as "the pillar and bulwark of the truth" (1 Tim 3:15; cf. 1 Pet 3:20). The Orthodox Church is also in agreement with Roman Catholics on the question of the *hierarchy,* as against the Protestant (though not the Anglican) view. Both Orthodox and Roman Catholic regard the office or priest and bishop as God-given institutions. But if they agree on the divine origin of the hierarchy, they manifest differing teachings on the extent of its power. Roman Catholics have elevated the bishop of Rome to the position of head of the whole Church. They have proclaimed not merely his primacy of jurisdiction but also his "infallibility *ex cathedra*" when he speaks on matters of faith and morals. This has been done at the sacrifice of the synodal system of the ancient Church and even to the detriment of the episcopal office. Here we should add that the Orthodox Church recognizes the primacy of honor of the Roman Pontiff as demonstrated by the rule and practice of the early Church, but ascribes infallibility only to the "pleroma," that is, the Church as a whole, and then to the hierarchy when it comes together in ecumenical councils as "the voice of the Church." According to the teaching of the Bible and the apostolic tradition, the Orthodox Church knows no other head of the Church than Christ himself.

On the question of the position of *the laity,* we can say that the Orthodox Church takes up its position between Roman Catholics and Protestants. She recognizes the rights of the laity in teaching, church administration, and the liturgy. This acknowledgment stems from her fidelity to the teaching of the Bible (1 Pet 2:9; Rev 1:6; 5:10) and patristic tradition on the laity as "a kingdom of priests" ($\beta \alpha \sigma i \lambda \epsilon \iota o \nu$ $i \epsilon \rho \acute{\alpha} \tau \epsilon \upsilon \mu \alpha$) and her belief in the efficacy of the power which is given in the sacraments of baptism and confirmation. In this way clergy and laity form *one* fellowship which is the mystical Body of Christ. The recognition of all these rights as inhering in the lay element in the Church has also made great progress in the Roman Catholic Church since the time of Pope John XXIII and has borne fruit in the Second Ecumenical Vatican Council. This has been the result of a revival of the biblical doctrine of the People of God rather than the influence of the Protestant doctrine of the general priesthood of the faithful, and as such has been much stressed in the recent revival of Orthodox theology in Greece. It has played a considerable role in the theological discussion of recent years in the Orthodox Church, in which Professor Panagiotis Trembelas, Father Hieronymus Kotsonis, and the author have taken some part.[29]

We referred above to the distinction between the Church militant and the Church triumphant; here we should add something about the relation which exists between these two parts of the Church as it is

29. Trembelas, *Die Laien in der Kirche,* 1950; H. Kotsonis, *Die Stellung der Laien im kirchlichen Organismus,* 1956; see the articles of P. Bratsiotis in the reviews *Anaplasis,* 1953, and *Gregorius Palamas,* 1955; see also Y. Congar, *Lay People in the Church,* Westminster, Md., 1965.

seen by Orthodox theologians. The relationship is established by prayer: the Church militant implores the intercession of the Church triumphant (the angels and saints), the Church triumphant prays for the Church militant, and both pray for the souls of those brothers who have died. According to our belief, the person of the Mother of God stands in a particularly close association with the Church as we can see was the case from the beginning from the Acts of the Apostles (see 1:14). Our dogmatic theology as well as our liturgy allots Mary a high place without, however, going beyond what we find in the apostolic tradition.

THE SACRAMENTS

In its teaching on the sacraments the Orthodox Church stands very much closer to the Roman than the Protestant position, excepting the Anglican High Church view from the latter. We limit ourselves here to the following brief comments:

1. According to the Orthodox view the sacraments are, by their nature, visible signs by means of which invisible grace is really communicated. In this we follow the teaching of Augustine. They are not just pledges of God's promises.

2. With regard to the conferring of the sacraments, the Orthodox Church believes, with John Chrysostom, that God communicates the sacraments invisibly through Christ. It is God who, as the true celebrant, confers the sacraments; the human priest is only his instrument. Accordingly, the priest, addressing the true celebrant in the great Eucharistic prayer, says, "It is you who are both the offerer and the offered." Likewise in the sacrament of baptism he does not say, "ego te baptizo" ("*I* baptize you"), but "the servant of God is baptized."

3. As regards the number of the sacraments, the Orthodox Church, at least since the thirteenth century, is at one with most Eastern Churches and Roman Catholics in accepting seven.

4. With regard to the form of administering the sacraments and their efficacy, there are many differences of opinion among the Churches which we cannot go into here except to mention the following points: (a) In the Orthodox Church *baptism* is administered by a threefold immersion in consecrated water of the one to be baptized, in keeping with the form of baptism in the primitive Church (Rom 6:4). (b) Again in keeping with early Christian practice, *confirmation* is administered directly after baptism. (c) Among the Orthodox the

Holy Eucharist is commonly received under both species. We agree
with Catholics that what is communicated is the true Body and Blood
of Christ, which results in a mystical union between Christ and the
communicant, in keeping with the early Christian way of speaking
of the latter as χριστοφόρος ("Christ-bearer") or θεοφόρος ("God-
bearer"). The communicant really bears Christ within him since,
according to the teaching of the early Church, Christ is truly present
in the most holy sacrament: bread and wine are changed into the
Body and Blood of Christ. (d) The Orthodox Church believes that,
as a result of sincere *repentance and penance,* absolute pardon and
forgiveness of sins are obtained. This implies that the penance im-
posed on the penitent by the priest has a purely pedagogical or
therapeutic value and cannot be considered as punishment or expiation. (e) The sacrament of *anointing* is administered in our Church
for the healing of bodily and spiritual infirmities (in accordance with
James 5:14) and not as a sacrament of the dying.

On the question of the *character indelebilis* ("the indelible seal")
of the sacraments of baptism, confirmation, and priestly ordination,
we should say that the Orthodox Church follows the ancient Fathers
such as Basil and Cyril of Jerusalem who speak of a seal (σφραγίς)
impressed on the one who receives them. The *Confession of Dositheus*
puts this teaching into practice.[30]

As for the question closely connected with this, *the validity of sacraments administered outside the Orthodox Church,* we should say that,
strictly speaking, they are not recognized. Nevertheless, in keeping
with its principle of *oikonomia* and in a spirit of brotherly compliance again modeled on the primitive Church, our Church has, in ex-
ceptional cases, recognized the baptism and priestly orders of Roman
Catholics, and often also the Lutheran baptism, of those who join
her. This was the case with the German princess Sophia von Hohen-
zollern, the sister of Kaiser Wilhelm II, the bride of the then crown
prince who was later to be King Constantine, and also with Princess
Frederika, the bride of the crown prince who was later to be King
Paul, when both embraced the Orthodox faith. Anna-Maria, the present queen of Greece, was also received into the Orthodox Church in
much the same way.

With regard to *Anglican orders,* the Ecumenical and Alexandrian
Patriarchates, the latter under Patriarch Meletios, and, following their
example, the Patriarchates of Jerusalem and Rumania, have expressed

30. P. Trembelas, *Dogmatik,* III, pp. 24–27.

their recognition in principle but have not been followed by the Churches of Russia, Greece, Serbia, and Bulgaria. Twenty-seven years ago the Greek Church was asked its point of view on this question by the then Archbishop of Canterbury and Anglican primate, Cosmo Lang. The Holy Synod passed this inquiry on to the theological faculty of the University of Athens, which after a thorough discussion of the question gave the following official answer which was confirmed by the Holy Synod (in 1939).[31]

Strictly speaking [κατ᾿ ἀκρίβειαν] the Orthodox Church recognizes as valid only the sacraments which are celebrated and conferred by her; but in special cases the Church can recognize the orders of an Anglican who enters the Orthodox Church, in keeping with her principle of ecclesiastical "oikonomia," when after careful examination she deems it expedient and proper.

In addition, the Holy Synod ruled that the competence to decide such an important question belonged only to *the Orthodox Church as a whole.*

In the years since this decision was given (1939–1965) not only has no progress been made toward the recognition of Anglican orders, but the reticence of the Greek Church has reinforced the attitude of the Churches of Russia, Serbia, Bulgaria, and other regions and, to judge by the acts of the Orthodox Church Congress of Moscow in 1948, has even influenced the churches of Alexandria and Rumania.[32] Even if Roman Catholic and Anglican orders were to be recognized, however, this would not imply an acceptance in principle of so-called intercommunion, which is strictly forbidden in the Orthodox Church. The question of the validity of Anglican ordination was placed by the Pan-Orthodox Synod of Rhodes (1961) on the agenda of subjects to be discussed.

The Orthodox Church holds firmly to the principle first enunciated by Cyprian, "extra ecclesiam nulla salus" ("outside the Church there is no salvation"). We may, nevertheless, suppose that, just as the salvation of the good thief and the descent of the Holy Spirit on Cornelius before his baptism (Acts 10:1–31) do not take away the fact, which is a truth of faith, that only the baptized can be saved, so in the same

31. The decision of the theological faculty of the University of Athens emerged, not from the discussions carried out at the relevant sessions, but from the detailed memoranda prepared by Professors Alivisatos, Balanos, and Bratsiotis and a briefer note of Professor Trembelas. See the official publication of the Holy Synod entitled *The Validity of Anglican Orders* (in Greek), Athens, 1939.

32. P. Bratsiotis, *Die anglikanischen Weihen,* 1966².

way the mercy of God who searches the heart of man can achieve its purpose in its own way, and this without taking away the fact that the Church is necessary for salvation.[33]

ESCHATOLOGY

The Orthodox Church holds not only a general final judgment but also a provisional individual judgment which takes place immediately after death and determines the eternal destiny of the deceased. It also believes in an *interim state* for the souls who await the resurrection of their bodies so that, once reunited to them, they may be present at the final judgment.[34] In this interim state, which begins with the individual judgment and will last to the second coming of the Lord, the souls of both righteous and sinners enjoy their reward or suffer their punishment respectively, even though the general judgment has not taken place. It is then that the definitive sentence of either reward or punishment is pronounced. The righteous, who are honored as saints in both Orthodox and Roman Catholic Churches as they were in the early Church, now belong in some way to the Church triumphant in heaven. They receive the prayers of intercession of the Church militant and bring them before God.

We Orthodox do not pray for "the poor souls" in purgatory. The idea of purgatory has always been foreign to our Church. From ancient times we have been content with the prayer of intercession for the souls of the departed which is read at the Eucharist and at special ceremonies of remembrance, the so-called *Mnemosynai,* which are held in connection with the giving of alms. Apart from the prayers of intercession for souls, we have twice a year a Vigil of All Souls, namely, before the "Sunday of abstinence from meat" ('Απόκρεω) and before Pentecost Sunday.

The Office of the Dead as celebrated in the Orthodox Church is distinguished by many moving prayers, hymns, and readings. It has a twofold purpose: the intercession for the souls of the departed and the admonition and consolation of the relatives and friends of the departed one who are there gathered together. The most beautiful of the hymns sung at this service are the highly lyrical compositions of

33. P. Trembelas, *Dogmatik,* II, p. 347.
34. See K. Dyobouniotis, *Der Zwischenzustand der Seelen,* 1904; J. Karmiris, 'Abriss der dogmatischen Lehre der Orthodoxen Kirche," in *Die Orthodoxe Kirche in griechischer Sicht,* 1959, I, pp. 112 ff.

the great Byzantine doctor of the Church John Damascene. In all eight tones of Byzantine church music they speak of the fearful mystery of death. It is characteristic of the special place of the Resurrection in Orthodox belief that in the office of the dead, sorrow is joined with Easter joy.

We should say finally that the expectation of the coming of the Lord has been kept alive throughout the centuries in the Orthodox Church: witness not only the Fathers of the Church and writers of the Byzantine Church but also the prayers of the liturgy.

Our Church only *hopes* that its prayers and intercession may be be some avail to those who have passed away. It accepts neither a purification for the souls of those in the interim state nor a period of punishment which will have an end nor a final reconstitution and reconciliation ($\grave{\alpha}\pi o\kappa\alpha\tau\acute{\alpha}\sigma\tau\alpha\sigma\iota\varsigma$ $\tau\hat{\omega}\nu$ $\pi\acute{\alpha}\nu\tau\omega\nu$). Despite the support of several Church Fathers and, in modern times, philosophical theologians and theological philosophers, especially in Russia, this teaching of Origen was condemned by the early Church at the fifth ecumenical council in 553.

BIBLIOGRAPHY

ST. ZANKOW, *Orthodoxes Christentum des Ostens,* Berlin, 1928; C. ANDROUTSOS, *Dogmatic Theology of the Orthodox Church* (in Greek), Athens, 1907; J. KARMIRIS, "Abriss der Dogmatischen Lehre der Orthodoxen Kirche," in P. BRATSIOTIS, *Die Orthodoxe Kirche in griechischer Sicht,* Stuttgart, 1959, I, pp. 112 ff; P. TREMBELAS, *Dogmatic Theology of the Orthodox Church,* (in Greek), 3 vols., Athens, 1958–1962; P. EVDOKIMOV, *L'Orthodoxie,* Paris, 1960; LE GUILLON, *L'esprit de l'Orthodoxie,* Paris, 1961; K. DYOBOUNIOTIS, *The Teaching of the Orthodox Church,* in *Ekklesia,* pp. 55–74; P. BRATSIOTIS, in *Die Autorität der Bibel heute* (a symposium brought together by the World Council of Churches), Zürich, 1951, pp. 19–33; B. VELLAS, "Die Heilige Schrift in der Griechisch-Orthodoxen Kirche," in *Die Orthodoxe Kirche in griechischer Sicht,* pp. 121–140.

ORTHODOX LITURGY

LITURGY is most intimately associated with faith; in it we have the encounter and union between the temporal and the eternal, the earthly and the heavenly. To begin with, "the architecture of a Christian place of worship is indissolubly bound up with the liturgy which takes place in it" and, moreover, "this architecture, deeply rooted in worship, must of its very nature be symbolical. . . . In this way every house of God is a symbol of the invisible, impalpable, supernatural reality of the mystical Body of Christ which is the Church"[1]—and "church" stands here not only for the Church in the abstract but also for the actual building. In the words of Blessed Maximus the Confessor, "the Church here on earth points to the glorified Church of the heavenly Jerusalem," and for Germanos, the seventh-century patriarch of Constantinople, the Church is "heaven on earth, being a place in which God himself dwells and moves." This is the message which is conveyed in a particularly clear way by the cupola of a Byzantine church which bears, in the center of the inner surface, an image of Christ as universal lord ($\pi\alpha\nu\tau\kappa\rho\acute{\alpha}\tau\omega\rho$). We read in a Byzantine hymn: "When we enter the temple of your glory, we believe that we are standing in heaven"; this exalted reflection corresponds to everything we find in a Byzantine church, especially the paintings. Everyone knows the important role of icons in Orthodox faith; they are the visible signs of the invisible presence of Christ, the Mother of God, the angels and saints—in short, of the Church triumphant. Increasingly during the last forty-five years Orthodox icons have been made the object of a thorough reevaluation, even of studies in speculative theology and by not only Orthodox students and thinkers but also those of other faiths. There has been talk of a "discovery" of their "soul" and even of a "theology of icons."[2]

The high point of Orthodox liturgy is the celebration of the Eucha-

1. Alexei Hackel, "Der Kirchenbau als Symbol," in *Der christliche Osten*, 1939, pp. 245–258.
2. Taking up an expression of the Russian Prince Eugene Trubetzkoy, the well-known Roman Catholic religious psychologist G. Wunderle speaks of "the discovery of icons" in his essay "Über die heiligen Ikonen," in *Der christliche Osten*, 1939, pp. 230 ff. The same scholar has put us in his debt with his fine study in religious psychology entitled *Über die Seele der heiligen Ikonen*, 1937. On the theology of icons see L. Koch in *Benediktinische Monatschrift*, 1937, vol. 11 ff, and H. Renges, *Die Bilder-lehre des heiligen Johannes von Damaskus*, 1938.

rist in which, in the words of the well-known Russian theologian Chomiakow, "the entire fullness of ecclesiastical teaching and the spirit of the Church finds expression . . . so that only he can understand the Church who grasps the meaning of its liturgy."[3] F. Heiler, who possesses a good knowledge of our Church and is favorable to it, makes this view his own when he writes: "The Eucharistic liturgy is the point of intersection of the whole life of the Church, the center of the sacraments which either prepare for it, are in dependence on it, or flow from it . . . the whole rich liturgy with all its visible ceremonies and moving prayers is like a wonderful garland which adorns this central mystery."[4] The Eucharist is also the center of the spirit of piety which is a special characteristic of the Orthodox Church. This piety is expressed in the mystery and symbolism of the church building which represents "the tabernacle of God" on earth and symbolizes the heavenly Jerusalem in its hymns, prayers, and all its liturgy. In the Eucharist the faithful experience the whole content of their faith and especially the mystery of Christ and mystical union with him who is their Lord. This union which is brought about in the Holy Eucharist is the whole purpose of the liturgy.

The entire course of the liturgical year revolves around this mystical center: the crucified and risen Christ. All the days of the year are dedicated to God; they all receive a blessing from this center and direct its rays to men. For this reason, following the Psalmist (Ps 65:11), we call the liturgical year "a garland of the bounties of the Lord." It is formed of the movable feasts, which depend for their date on Easter, and the fixed feasts of Christ, the Mother of God, and the saints. This "rich and powerful drama" which is played against the suggestive background of Byzantine church architecture has inspired a host of great poets in the Greek East and produced a rich and magnificent hymnography. This latter gives the Orthodox liturgy a most imposing character. As Kirchhoff says: "As in heaven the singing of the angels rings out and soars around the exalted majesty of God . . . in the same way the Eastern Church is convinced that the service she offers God's majesty is the same as that of the angels . . . that her hymns are modeled on those of the angels, an echo of the everlasting song of the cherubim."[5]

Our Church's liturgical year begins on September 1. It makes a

3. See his *Östliches Christentum,* ed. by Burnoff-Ehrenberg, 1925, p. 25.
4. F. Heiler, *Urkirche und Ostkirche,* pp. 287–288.
5. K. Kirchhoff, "Das heilige Jahr," in *Der christliche Osten,* 1939, p. 93.

circle around "the sun of justice" similar to the secular year based on the movement of the earth around the sun. Kirchhoff says: "Just as the sun bathes the earth in the rays which she sends out and bestows fertility and growth upon her, so the heavenly sun, Christ the giver of light and life, enters into the liturgical year of the Church of God with his gifts and the riches of his goodness in order to fill her with the divine light of his grace." The liturgical year is a reflection of the eternal icons, an image of them realized in space and time. It is divided into four interpenetrating and overlapping cycles: two annual, one weekly, and one daily. The first annual cycle is formed by the movable feasts which revolve around Easter, the greatest feast of the Orthodox Church and the culmination of the whole year. This cycle is divided into the so-called triodion period—which lasts ten weeks, begins with "Pharisee and Publican Sunday," and ends with the Great Saturday—and the Pentecostarion period, beginning at Easter and lasting eight weeks. The second annual cycle, which overlaps with the first, is formed of the cycle of immovable feasts of Christ, the Mother of God, and the saints of the twelve *Menaeai*. Intersecting these two annual cycles is the weekly cycle in the course of which the hymns of the Resurrection and Trinity are sung in one of the eight tones of Byzantine music, and a day is set aside for the remembrance of the Resurrection, the angels, John the Baptist, the betrayal of Jesus, the Apostles and Church leaders, the Passion of Christ, the martyrs, all the saints and the departed brethren. And, finally, we have *the daily cycle* of the so-called "hourly prayers" which follows its course within the other cycles.

We can summarize the main characteristics of Orthodox liturgy as follows:[6]

1. Its genuinely *ancient character,* recalling the oldest forms of Christian worship and preserving their essential elements.

2. Its *biblical character,* consisting in the rich use of texts taken from the Greek Bible and the preservation of its style and color. The biblical books most in use are the Book of Psalms and the Apocalypse,[7] although this latter is not officially allowed for liturgical use on account of its apparently chiliastic character and the difficulties of interpretation which it presents. The honor in which Holy Scripture

6. P. Trembelas, "Der Orthodoxe Kultus," in *Die Orthodoxe Kirche in griechischer Sicht,* 1959, I, pp. 157 ff.

7. I have tried to show this in my commentary; see P. Bratsiotis, *Commentary on the Apocalypse* (in Greek), 1950, pp. 50 ff, and my essay in *Festschrift für Prof. H. Clavier,* Strasbourg *(Revue d'Histoire et de Philosophie réligieuse),* 1962, pp. 116–121.

is held in the Orthodox liturgy can be seen from the fact that the priest or deacon, before reading from it, calls out "Σοφία" ("here is wisdom") and "πρόσχωμεν" ("let us listen attentively"), and also from the command to stand before the reading of the Gospel: "Let us listen to the holy Gospel standing on our feet." It is also characteristic of the Orthodox Church that in her liturgy the Scriptures have long been read in the vernacular. We should note finally that in the *Orthros,* or daily morning service, the New Testament, with the exception of the Apocalypse, is read in sequence; the Psalms are prayed in their entirety every week, divided into two sections, with the exception of the so-called *Kathismoi;* and we read passages selected from different books of the Old Testament at the Vesper service of many feast days, especially during the great fast which precedes Easter.[8]

3. Its *strongly theological character,* influenced deeply as it is by the main trinitarian, Christological, and ecclesiological truths of faith. This has influenced not only the liturgy but also Byzantine architecture and painting and, in particular, the rich and splendid hymnography of the Eastern Church. The liturgy bears the mark of the Resurrection of the Lord in a quite unique way, and this mystery of faith has put its stamp on the whole liturgical year.

4. Orthodox liturgy is strongly *symbolical, mystagogical,* and *transcendental,* to which we may add, with Bulgakow, its *cosmic* character.[9] The whole cycle of the year is consecrated to God; by means of the liturgy sanctification comes not only upon men but on all created things and all creatures in the cosmos, whose eager longing is directed to the revelation of the children of God, since even irrational creation has to be freed from that subjection from which the children of God have already escaped: "We know that the whole creation has been groaning in travail together until now" (Rom 8:22). Paul is speaking here of a redemptive process which reaches its culmination in "the new heavens and the new earth." All of this is not only attested to in liturgical texts and hymns but is reflected in Byzantine church architecture and painting. All of these form the common inheritance of all the Orthodox Churches. With their help the souls of the faithful pass from the earthly to the heavenly world and unite themselves in

8. A. Rahlfs, *Die alttestamentlichen Lektionen der Griechischen Kirche,* 1915; P. Bratsiotis, "Das Alte Testament in der Orthodoxen Kirche," in *Trierer Theologische Zeitschrift,* 1960.

9. S. Bulgakow, *L'Orthodoxie,* pp. 42 ff.

spirit with the Church triumphant. This is stated explicitly in the great Eucharistic Prayer of Thanksgiving of the liturgies of Basil and Chrysostom which conclude with the "Holy, Holy, Holy": "Together with these holy and heavenly powers we say: 'O Thou Lord and lover of men, thou art holy and all-holy. . . .' "

5. Trembelas also stresses *the sacrificial aspect of the divine liturgy,* since its center is the unbloody sacrifice of expiation of the Redeemer who freely gave his life for the life of men.

6. The *communal character* which our liturgy has in common with that of Roman Catholics is expressed in a special way in the celebration of the Eucharist, for example, in the following dialogues: the deacon commands, "Let us make our requests in the peace of the Lord," and the people answer with the *Kyrie eleison;* the priest cries, "Peace be with you!" and the people answer, "And with your spirit"; the deacon says, "Let us love one another so that we may with one mind profess our faith," and the people answer, "The Father, the Son, and the Holy Spirit: the Trinity of Persons equal in nature and indivisible"; the priest calls out, "Let us lift up our hearts," and the people answer, "We have already lifted them up"; and so on. Apart from this, the communal character of the Orthodox liturgy is shown in a very special way in the manner in which holy communion is administered. All drink from the same chalice by using the same spoon, and all communicate under both species. This also explains why the Eucharist may not be celebrated in the Orthodox Church without the presence of the congregation.

7. The celebration of the Eucharist in the Orthodox Church and the Orthodox liturgy in general have a charismatic (pneumatic) dimension. To be sure, they make use of many media which appeal to the senses—poetry, vocal music (without organ), painting (but no sculpture)—but the spiritual character of the liturgy is preserved and strengthened by keeping the profane firmly in its place. To quote Zankow once again: "Orthodox liturgy is not fond of noise and bustle; it prefers the inner sanctuary, the church, and avoids the hustle of the outside world . . . it is a liturgy which preserves a balance between the earthly and the heavenly, between content and form."[10]

8. The *didactic character* of the liturgy is strengthened by the full use of biblical readings, prayers, hymns—especially in the liturgy of the Eucharist—and particularly by the sermon, which has been rehabil-

10. S. Zankow, *Orthodoxes Christentum des Ostens,* p. 109.

itated and strengthened in the last few decades as one of the most educative elements of the liturgy. it is true that the Orthodox Church has been reproached with being predominantly a "cultic community" to the detriment of the sermon and the charismatic element.[11] We do not deny that our Church is a cultic community, but we do deny that she is that and nothing more. Perhaps I may close this chapter by quoting the words of F. Heiler:

The Eastern Church is a sacramental church, and yet at the same time a church of the Word in the fullest sense. Its liturgical year is itself a sermon on the mystery of divine love, and this sermon is preached in words more powerful and sublime than any that could come from the mouth of a preacher. This mystery which is expressed in the words of the Apostle: ". . . the preaching of Jesus Christ, according to the revelation of the mystery which was kept secret for long ages but is now disclosed . . . [Rom 16:25]."[12]

BIBLIOGRAPHY

H. ALVISATOS, "Der Kultus der Orthodoxen Kirche," in *Ekklesia,* ed. F. S. SCHULTZE, pp. 91–99; P. TREMBELAS, "Der Orthodoxe Gottesdienst," in *Die Orthodoxie Kirche in griechischer Sicht,* I, pp. 157–168; G. SOTIRIOU, "Die Kunst in der Griechisch-Orthodoxen Kirche," *ibid.,* II, pp. 175–191; D. PSARIANOS, "Die byzantinische Musik," *ibid.,* II, pp. 155–174.

11. Against this view see D. Balanos, *Is the Orthodox Church just a Cultic Community?* (in Greek), 1909.
12. See his *Urkirche und Ostkirche,* pp. 363 f.

THE ETHOS OF THE ORTHODOX CHURCH

THE ETHOS of a church is intimately connected with its faith and liturgy; it is bound to have a thoroughly religious character. If it is legitimate to speak of a Roman Catholic, a Protestant, or an Orthodox faith and liturgy, then it must be equally legitimate to speak of their ethos, since it is nothing else than the expression and result of the kind of faith and liturgy which each church has. One of the main forms of expression and characteristics of this ethos will be piety. If to be like God is represented as the purpose of the creation of man, then the divinization of man must be the final end of both the Incarnation of the Word and the existence of the Church which finds expression in its ethos. The divinization of man will therefore be for the Orthodox Church the center of its ethos. The essential nature of this ethos will be defined as the imitation of Christ as the means to this end.

With regard to the piety of the Orthodox Church and its ethos, the accusation has been made, from both the Protestant (e.g., Harnack) and the Catholic side (e.g., Steffes), that it is too much preoccupied with the ascetical side and too prone to despise the world as the result of an exclusive orientation to the life to come. These critics speak of a lack of energy and interest in moral issues. We shall be speaking later about the position of the Orthodox Church with regard to the world and the good things it contains. For the moment we will say just this, that our Church is inspired in its encounter with the world by the spirit and living example of the primitive Church which saw life in terms of struggle. It shows neither more nor less reserve with regard to the world than the Apostles and the early Church in general; it turns, not against the world *as such,* but against sin which prevails in this world. The Church preserves that faith which overcomes the world, together with hope and charity, for no other purpose than to save the world, since this is, according to the Gospel, the whole purpose of the mission of Christ (Matt 5:13 ff; John 3:15 ff; 8:12 ff). The imitation of Christ is, as we have seen, essential to a Christian ethos and, at the same time, the way toward the final end of the divinization of man (Matt 11:29; John 8:12; 1 Cor 11:1; 1 Pet 3:22–24). We may recall here the saying of Ignatius: "Since we have become his apprentices, let us

55

live as becomes Christians."[1] The way of thinking and living characteristic of Orthodoxy is *ascetical* and *mystical* and is taken from the
early Church. According to this way of thinking, divine grace works in
unison with the human will. As a result of this, the following are the
main virtues inculcated in the Orthodox Church:

1. A *piety* which strives toward the ideal of *theosis* (divinization)
yet goes hand in hand with a profound *humility* before God and one's
fellowmen. Isaac of Syria identifies humility with perfection; to the
question "What is perfection?" he answered, "the depths of humility."

2. A *perseverance* under persecution and suffering for the name of
Christ which remains full of hope and joy and stands firm even to the
point of martyrdom.

3. A basic attitude which is both ascetical and mystical, understood,
not as aversion from the world, but *vigilance,* self-conquest, and *overcoming the world* in order to realize the ideal of sanctity on the personal and moral level. According to Heiler this ideal is "that of the
early Christians which combined profound humility and a great readi-
ness to suffer with divine joy and all-embracing love."[2] In elaborating
further on this ideal of holiness Heiler refers to the classical words
of Cyril of Jerusalem, words that provide the best explanation of the
answer which the congregation makes to the cry of the priest before
communion—Τὰ ἅγια τοῖς ἁγίοις ("the Holy [Reality] to the holy
[people]")—when he announces the *mysterium tremendum:*[3]

In truth, there is but one who is Holy; holy, that is, by nature.
If we are holy we are so not by nature but by participation, ex-
ercise, and prayer.[4]

The many fast days which are observed, together with the rich
variety of prayers accompanying them, bear out this ascetical-mystical
spirit of the Orthodox Church and at the same time promote it. These
fast days, most of which go back to the early Church,[5] may be enu-
merated as follows:

a. Each Wednesday and Friday, in memory of the betrayal and
crucifixion of the Lord.

b. The forty days' fast of Advent.

1. *Magn.,* 92 and especially 101.
2. F. Heiler, *op. cit.,* p. 549.
3. "The fearful mystery"—a phrase used by Rudolph Otto in his work *The Idea
of the Holy* (New York, 1958).
4. *Myst. Cat.,* 5, 19.
5. See K. Holl, "Die Entstehung der vier Fastenzeiten in der griechischen Kirche,"
in *Gesammelte Aufsatze zur Kirchengeschichte,* II, 1928, pp. 157 ff.

c. The great and strict fast before Easter which begins with what we call "cheese week"[6] and lasts eight weeks.

d. The short and movable fast before the great Feast of the Apostles on June 29. This fast begins shortly after Pentecost week.

e. Two fasts which closely follow each other: the first from August 1 to 6 (before the Feast of the Transfiguration of Christ[7]), the second from August 7 to 15 (before the Feast of the Assumption of the Mother of God).

f. The strict fast on the Feast of the Martyrdom of St. John the Baptist, August 29.

g. The strict fast on the great Feast of the Cross, September 14 this feast is in memory of the finding of the true cross).

4. Humility is the strong foundation of the Christian virtues as is shown in the Beatitudes (Matt 5:3).

5. The main characteristic, the crown and fulfillment of the Christian way of life, is, however, love in its dual form of love of God and love of neighbor. This is the reflection of and the answer to the antecedent and immeasurable love of God for men, the love which became incarnate in Jesus Christ.[8] In keeping with its biblical and anthropological suppositions, the Orthodox Church holds that this dual love is innate in man who is created in the image of God, but that this image has been obscured, but not entirely destroyed, by sin. In order that it may be restored and developed, the charismatic assistance of divine grace is necessary (Gen 1:25; Rev 17:26, 29; 1 Thess 4:9). This message of love is already present in the words of Antigone: οὔτοι συνέχθειν ἀλλὰ συμφιλεῖν ἔφυν ("I am not here to hate but to love others").

The fulfillment of this divine commandment of love must be seen, with Paul (1 Cor 12:3 ff), as possible only by the gift of God. In any case, humility and love are so intimately connected in Orthodox ascetic theology that the one is unthinkable without the other. We may go further and say that the one is the touchstone of the genuineness of the other, and indeed of all the Christian virtues.

The author, who is himself a member of the Orthodox Church, must leave the answer to the question how far this ideal has been put into practice among us to the conscientious judgment and good will

6. So-called because the faithful cannot eat flesh meat during this week, only cheese and eggs.

7. On this feast one may eat fish but neither meat, eggs, nor cheese.

8. Matt 5:43 ff; John 13:35; Rom 13:8 ff; Gal 6:2.

of those who have a genuine knowledge of our Church. He may be permitted to refer the reader once again to Heiler[9] and to remind him of the charity shown throughout the history of the Byzantine Church, the history of Balkan Christians during that centuries-long servitude, and finally the history of the Russian Church, at least in the last half-century.

I may be allowed to conclude this chapter by stating my view as an Orthodox theologian on the well-known eros-agape theory of the distinguished Swedish theologian Bishop Nygren.[10] Nygren posited an irreconcilable opposition between Christian agape and Platonic eros by basing himself on the Lutheran doctrine of the complete depravation of human nature through original sin and the Lutheran opposition to Greek philosophy. He was also anxious to extend the well-known theory of Adolph Harnack on the falsification of the primitive Christian message of the New Testament by the philosophers to the field of primitive Christian ethics, and concluded that the true idea of Christian love was falsified because of the influence of Platonic eros-philosophy on the theology of the Christian East and of Augustine. But while, according to Nygren, the way of divine love toward men—which alone makes it possible for us to love God and men—has nothing to do with Platonic eros directed toward God, Orthodox theology has to remember that besides this supernatural way there is also another way, that of love for God and men. This way must be appreciated and taken seriously into account, the more so that it is known to the Old Testament and to Jesus Christ himself.[11]

Here may I add that in my own studies of the Old Testament I have found traces of a quite clearly defined mysticism, as have other Old Testament scholars. One example would be Psalm 63, characterized by Franz Delitzsch as "a spiritual love song."[12]

The Orthodox view of divine eros finds radical expression in the writings of the Byzantine mystic Simeon, called "the New Theologian," and in her hymnography, and has been formed under the influ-

9. See his overall judgment on the Eastern Church in *op. cit.*, pp. 545 ff.

10. A. Nygren, *Eros and Agape,* London, 1953[2]; B. Joannides, *Das neue Gebot der Liebe,* 1950; P. Bratsiotis, *Der Sinn der christlichen Liebe,* 1956.

11. Lev 19:8; Deut 6:5; Matt 22:40 cf. Rom 8:31; 1 Cor 2:9; 8:1, 3; 13:1 ff.

12. See R. Kittel, *Die Psalmen,* pp. 144, 233 ff, 270, where he speaks of an Israelite mysticism formed under the influence of the Prophets; see also J. Ziegler. *Liebe Gottes bei den Propheten,* 1930, p. 116.

ence of Origen[13] and several other Fathers of the Church.[14] Theodore Studites speaks in one of his "ecclesiastical Psalms of Ascent" of "the wingbeat of divine eros." This divine eros finds expression in Christian asceticism and martyrdom.

We would agree with the Roman Catholic philosopher J. Hessen against Nygren when he says that Platonic eros and Christian agape are indeed different but intimately connected and that they *both* form part of a complete human nature.

13. For example, in his *Homilies on the Canticle,* edited by Dom Rousseau, *Sources Chrétiennes,* Vol. 37, Paris, 1953.

14. Methodius, Gregory of Nyssa, Pseudo-Dionysius, Maximus Confessor, John Climacus, and others.

MONASTICISM IN THE ORTHODOX CHURCH

THE ETHOS, and indeed the whole spirit, of the Orthodox Church has impressed itself on Orthodox monasticism, which is in direct continuity with the monastic institutions of the early Church and bears the mark of the ascetic and organizing genius of Basil the Great who has also exerted influence on Western monasticism. This explains the contemplative character of the Orthodox Church in general, a characteristic which has been acknowledged and highly praised by notable Roman Catholic scholars such as K. Lübeck and G. Wunderle and even by Protestant students of the Eastern Church such as K. Holl and F. Heiler. We find in the Orthodox Church not only a continuation of the ancient monastic communities but also the most primitive form of monasticism, which is the anchorite state practiced by hermits.

Throughout the whole history of the Orthodox Church Mount Athos has been the chief center and stronghold of monasticism, a fact well illustrated recently by the millenary celebration of its foundation. Here the ancient Eastern monastic tradition, originating in Egypt, spreading throughout Palestine, Syria, Cappadocia, Bithynia, and Constantinople, came to be concentrated in the course of time and was thus preserved down to the present. Here also the practice of the so-called *hesychasm*,[1] which has become a characteristic of Orthodox monasticism, was elaborated and systematized. The twenty monasteries of this holy mountain, which together form in some way an independent and well-organized monastic republic, with the monastery of Karyae at the head, have for ten centuries been of great service to all the Orthodox Churches and peoples in the religious, moral, and cultural fields. Moreover, as is generally acknowledged, this spiritual republic has exerted a beneficial influence even beyond the boundaries of the Orthodox world, especially in the West. This was demonstrated at the stirring Pan-Orthodox and Pan-Christian celebration of the first thousand years of Mount Athos in which Western Christianity also took part with enthusiasm; in fact, the celebration took place not

---

1. A way of practicing concentration and meditation based on a special technique of breathing and the recital of a short "Jesus-prayer."

61

merely on the holy mountain but also within the boundaries of the Western Church, in Venice.[2]

The celebrations which took place on the holy mountain in the presence of the leader and representative of all the Orthodox Churches and of many friends from the West provided much food for thought, especially on the present downward trend in Orthodox monasticism, the reasons which have led to this, and the possible means for overcoming the crisis. The Orthodox world lives in hope of a spiritual renewal which must take the form of a carefully planned reorganization of monasticism—which all admit to be absolutely essential—backed by a greater solicitude for this ancient and important institution on the part of all the Orthodox Churches. To this end the sources of that enthusiasm which characterized the early Church have to be revitalized. It would be a disaster for the whole Church, not just for monasticism, if the appreciation of what this way of life means to the Church were allowed to die out.

BIBLIOGRAPHY

A. HARNACK, *Das Mönchtum, seine Ideale und seine Geschichte,* 1906[3]; K. HOLL, *Über das griechische Mönchtum, Gesammelte Aufsätze,* II, 1928, pp. 270–292; F. HEILER, *Urkirche und Ostkirche,* pp. 365–389; A. THEODOROU, "Das Mönchtum der Ostkirche," in *Die Orthodoxe Kirche in griechischer Sicht,* II, pp. 70–91; B. STEPHANIDES, "Das Mönchtum in Geschichte und Gegenwart," *Ekklesia,* X, 1939, pp. 100 ff.

2. We should mention specially the participation of the Benedictines of Chevetogne in Belgium, and Maria Laach represented by Father Chrysostam Dahm. A very fine volume commemorating the event has been published by the Benedictine Monastery of Chevetogne, entitled: *Le millénaire du Mont Athos, Etudes et Mélanges,* 2 vols., 1963–1965.

THE CONSTITUTION OF THE ORTHODOX CHURCH

THE PARTICULAR ethos and spirit of the Orthodox Church is also impressed on its organization and canon law, which form a connecting link between all the individual churches. A characteristic note of these churches, seen from the institutional point of view, is their *democratic basis,* and this they took from the primitive Church. This democratic character is based on the Gospel but can also be traced back to some extent to Greek influence. Like the early Church before the division, the Orthodox Church is composed of clergy and laity, with monks forming a group between the two. Clergy, monks, and laity together form the pleroma (the fullness) of the Church, whose unity is both symbolized in and guaranteed by the office of bishop. The democratic constitution of the Orthodox Church is clearly shown in its system of synods and councils as well as in the autocephalous principle (independent government of the individual member Churches). At the head of each bishopric composed of clergy, monks, and laity is the bishop; at the head of each autocephalous Church is its primate with his synod of bishops; and, finally, the ecumenical patriarch is at the head of all the Orthodox Churches as "primus inter pares" of all the bishops. The highest authority in the Church is, however, the ecumenical council composed of all the bishops which decides all questions concerning faith, liturgy, and Church law.

The hierarchy gathered together in council is, therefore, the bearer of the highest authority in the Church and constitutes the voice of the Church. But the democratic spirit of the Orthodox Church comes strongly to the fore at this point, since recognition of the infallibility even of conciliar decisions is reserved to the whole pleroma of the Church in which the Holy Spirit sent by Christ dwells (John 14:26; 15:26). It is in the entire body of the Church that the so-called consciousness of the Orthodox Church resides as an infallible witness; hence any conciliar decision—even if coming from an ecumenical council—is invalid if not accepted and recognized by this universal

63

Church consciousness. This explains, *inter alia,* the disapproval and rejection of the so-called "Robber Council" at Ephesus (449) and the Council of Florence (1439). In any event, we have in our Church no infallible or absolute primate, since, as we said, the ecumenical patriarch, both juridically and in historical fact, is accepted as "primus inter pares" among the bishops and nothing more.

The *canon law* of the Orthodox Church, which is based on the sacred canons (norms of law) and forms with the profession of faith and liturgy the common link between the individual churches, regulates both internal matters and relations with those outside the Church. When, however, we come to the relations between each autocephalous Church and the national state in which it is located, another factor enters into play which is not entirely independent of canon law. We shall deal with this question in a later chapter on the relations between Church and state.

BIBLIOGRAPHY

N. MILASCH, *Das Kirchenrecht der morgenländischen Kirche,* 1905[2]; H. ALIVISATOS, "Das kanonische Recht der Orthodoxen Kirche," *Ekklesia,* X, 1939, pp. 57–90; H. KOTSONIS, "Verfassung und Aufbau der Orthodoxen Kirche," in *Die Orthodoxe Kirche in griechischen Sicht,* I, pp. 169 ff; II, pp. 92–115.

ATTITUDE OF THE ORTHODOX CHURCH TO THE WORLD

OBJECTIONS are raised against the Orthodox Church from different angles: she disregards or even hates the present world and gives her attention exclusively to the supernatural and the life to come. To this accusation we can reply with arguments from Scripture, the Fathers of the Church, the liturgy and hymnography of the Church, and, in fact, the entire history of the Church to the effect that the attitude of the Orthodox Church to the world and culture—whether understood of material civilization or in the spiritual and moral sense—is in the main not essentially different from the attitude of the united Catholic Church of the first eight centuries. This attitude was not one of wholesale acceptance or rejection; we could characterize it as one of prudent appraisal. Such a stance could be supported by many New Testament texts; it certainly dominated the attitude of the early Church and the writings of countless Fathers of the Church, and in fact is a part of every higher form of religion.

Every religion—and in particular Christianity, the spiritual religion *par excellence*—manifests an intense movement toward the otherworldly. Every religion seeks to free men from the fetters of this world and imprisonment in matter so that he may turn to God. As Augustine so pointedly says: "Our heart is restless till it rests in Thee." This means that there must be a certain tension in the relations between Christianity and culture. The problem can be solved in one of two ways: distance (that means, in practice, asceticism and flight from the world) or synthesis. The history of both the undivided Church and the Orthodox Church gives us more examples of synthesis than of distance.

There are many scriptural texts which speak in otherworldly terms and suggest *distance*. Among others, we may mention the words of Jesus recorded in Matthew 6:25; 16:24–26; John 18:36; and Paul's words in 1 Corinthians 7:8; Philippians 3:8–20 (cf. Heb 13:14); and finally the New Testament texts, especially in Paul and the Johan-

65

nine writings, which speak of "the world" as under the influence of evil and sin[1] and condemn friendship with the world understood in this sense (1 John 2:15 ff; James 4:4 ff).

At the same time, many texts can also be found in favor of *synthesis*, among them the command addressed to the first man and woman: "Increase and multiply and subdue the earth" (Gen 1:28). Support can also be found in the preaching of Jesus, especially his parables—the sower, the net, the leaven in the dough (see Matt 13 and parallels in the other Synoptics), the talents (Matt 25 and Luke 19). He speaks of his and his Father's love for the world (John 3:16; cf. 1 John 2:2; 4:9; Rom 8:32), and there are, finally, his last instructions to his disciples before they begin their mission (Matt 28:19 f; 16:1 ff; cf. also John 10:16).

Over and above these sayings, however, we have the example of Jesus. He was indifferent to material things without at the same time renouncing the use of them, and, moreover, he did not give his attention primarily to the material needs of his people. He proclaimed the supremacy of spiritual values while at the same time he placed himself at the service of men, sanctifying labor by taking up a profession and blessing married life and the family.

We also have the teaching and example of the Apostles, who likewise were imbued with the spirit of asceticism in the sense of subduing the body and subordinating bodily needs to the life of the Spirit (Gal 5:24). At the same time they combated a dualist type of asceticism (Col 2:13; 1 Tim 4:3; cf. Rom 14:14; 1 Cor 8:7 ff) even as they exposed the wisdom of this world as foolishness (1 Cor 1:20 ff; 2:14) and sought to protect the faithful from the deception of worldly philosophy (Col 2:8). Yet they did not at all reject the use of cultural values in the service of the Gospel.

With only few exceptions this approach initiated by Jesus was followed by the apologists and early Church Fathers and, we can say, by the whole Catholic Church of the first eight centuries. They sought for a synthesis between Christianity and Greco-Roman culture, never however in an uncritical way but mindful of the warnings of St. Paul[2] and conscious that the faithful in this present, transitory life were citizens of two worlds, the present world and the world to come. This consciousness is strikingly expressed in the Epistle to Diognetus (5:5 ff):

1. John 7:17; 15:18 ff; 16:11; 17:9, 14; Rom 5:12; Gal 1:4; 1 Cor 1:20; Eph 5:10; 6:12; Tit 2:12; cf. Matt 4:8; James 1:17; 3:6.
2. See 1 Cor 2:15; 7:29 ff; 2 Cor 16:10; 1 Thess 5:21.

Christians dwell in their own native countries but only in the manner of wayfarers. As citizens they take part in everything, yet as if they were strangers. Every foreign country is their fatherland, yet their own fatherland is foreign to them . . . . They maintain themselves on this earth, but they are citizens of heaven.

This critical attitude to the world, maintained in the Orthodox Church, allows for a prudent cooperation between the Church and culture, between the Church and the world in general. The Church must seek to penetrate into the world of culture to be, as it were, the soul in the body, the yeast in the dough, to give it a new form and sanctify it, and she has to do this without making "the way of the world" her own (Rom 12:2). And so, despite protests and reactionary movements especially from monastic and sectarian groups, the Church has helped preserve the splendid Byzantine or Greco-Christian culture of the East intact down to the present day. Of course, monks also took part in this: their knowledge and preservation of classical literature, copying of ancient Greek manuscripts, poetry, painting, music, their defense of icons, should all be mentioned here apart from their other achievements. In addition, the imposing edifice of Western medieval culture grew out of a combination of Christianity with Greco-Roman culture, though elements of the cultural life of the West itself were also assimilated. Together with that of Byzantium, Western medieval culture built the bridge from ancient classical times to the dawn of the modern age. Even under the Turkish yoke and even in Russia the Orthodox Church preserved this tradition of a synthesis between Greek and Christian culture, though this was specially in evidence in the territory of the Ecumenical Patriarchate.

To sum up, we can say that the attitude of the Orthodox Church to culture and the world in general proceeds neither by capitulation nor domination. Rather, as we have said, its whole effort is directed to a penetration into the world with the purpose of transforming and sanctifying it. The ancient Greek liturgies, especially that of St. Basil, give us a very faithful reflection of this attitude. Here the Church prays not only for the fertility of the earth, for various categories such as artisans and pilgrims, but also for the strengthening of kings "that the Lord may inspire their hearts to do good to the Church and the people." Prayers are said also for the people that their stores may be full of all good things, for the education of the young, the consolation of the elderly, the defense of orphans and widows, the deliverance of those in prison, the healing of the sick. There are, finally, prayers for the blessing and consecration of houses and vineyards and for all sorts of things pertaining to the life and cultural activity of the people. All of this proves that this assessment of the Orthodox Church's attitude is justified.

Last but not least, we must mention, in discussing this topic, the priceless achievement of the Orthodox Church through centuries of history in Christianizing, civilizing, and even bringing into existence so many nations and peoples. This was done in spite of the fact that Barbarians were continually invading and even occupying her territory. In this part of the world it was Orthodox Christians who opened up new lands and, by giving the first impetus to writing, laid the foundations for national literatures and cultures. They succeeded also in preserving among the occupied nations of the East not only the Orthodox faith but their language, customs, and national consciousness. We can therefore state the attitude of the Orthodox Church to the world briefly as follows: she maintains the tradition of the early Church before the division. Stated negatively, this means that she avoids the extremes of secularism on the one hand and renunciation of the world on the other; stated positively, she strives to give the world a soul, a principle of life. As the Epistle to Diognetus (6:1) puts it: "What the soul is in the body, that is what Christians are in the world." Also included in the concept of "world" are, of course, modern science, art, and technology; these too have to be given life by the Church.

BIBLIOGRAPHY

P. BRATSIOTIS, *Christianity and Culture,* 1940 (in Greek); *Christianity and Humanism,* 1955 (in Greek); *Christianity and Technology,* 1960 (in Greek); N. LOUVARIS, "Kirche und Welt," in *Die Orthodoxe Kirche in griechischer Sicht,* II, pp. 144, 154.

ORTHODOX CHURCH AND NATION

WHAT WE HAVE SAID of the attitude of the Church to the world applies also, *mutatis mutandis,* to its understanding of the national state. For the state also is a part or an element of the world and, at the same time, a contributory factor in the formation of the world. In many cases the nation grows and develops with the Church and is animated by her—or at least ought to be. On this subject, Harnack's reproach against the Orthodox Church that nationalism has eaten into her like woodworm has been widely voiced since the beginning of the century, especially in the West. I became familiar with this charge while I was studying in Germany, especially by reading his book *The Essence of Christianity* and the paper which he wrote for the Prussian Academy of the Sciences entitled "The Spirit of the Western Church" (1913). I must confess that a reading of these two works left me somewhat upset and even astonished since the attack came not from a Roman Catholic, whose Church has always had a marked ecumenical character, but from a great scholar who belonged to a Protestant state church, and one which at that time had a strongly nationalist orientation. I was somewhat reassured when I learned that Harnack came from a province whose German population had suffered considerably from the Russian rule in force at that time. Shortly afterwards the First World War broke out; this war and its consequences opened the eyes of the Christian world to the dangers of the Satanic, uncontrolled power of nationalism and its insidious penetration into the life of the Church. And there were some Protestant theologians of note who did not escape the baneful influence of this spirit of nationalism.

In 1937 the world conference for practical Christianity was held at Oxford under the rubric "State, Nation, and Church." The very theme was a direct result of the extreme consequences of nationalism. As a full-time member of the ecumenical movement in Greece I had a part to play in the preparation of this congress. The leading figure in the work of preparation was, however, Dr. Hans Schönfeld, whose scientific and ecumenical activity was, unfortunately, brought to an early and untimely end. I had already published some contributions toward the work of the congress and had taken part in regional conferences in Yugoslavia: at Herzeg Novi in 1936 and Novisad in 1937. At the former of these I had read a paper entitled "State, Nation, Church: An Orthodox Viewpoint" which was later published at Berne in the review *Internationale kirchliche Zeitschrift*.[1] Because of the rather bold views expressed in it, this paper was the occasion of a brisk and sustained debate with some of my older colleagues in the theological faculty of Athens in the pages of *Ekklesia*, the official publication of the Greek synod. It is necessary to add that I was the official representative of our Church at the Oxford World Congress. I give here a summary of this paper and take the occasion of developing some of the arguments contained in it.

In the first place, the nation is a very important aspect or element of the world animated by the Church. It consists of a group of men who share the same origins and history and often the same language and religion. In this last case the bond between the individual members of the whole is at its strongest. It is perfectly natural and understandable that Christianity, based as it is on Scripture and committed to following the example of Jesus and the Apostles, should give the same attention to and show the same interest in such a collectivity as it does for each individual person. In the Old Testament Israel is chosen from all nations as "the possession of Yahweh's . . . a kingdom of priests, a holy nation" (Ex 19:5–6). The history of this people is the principal theme of the Old Testament writings; it is a history in the course of which the people are led on and educated by divine love and care as a preparation for the redemption of mankind in Jesus Christ. Although sharply distinguished from the Chosen People, the other nations do not cease to be the object of the loving providence of God enlightening them with many rays emanating from the *Logos spermatikos*[2] and destining them for conversion by means of Israel and the coming Messiah.

In the Old Testament Moses and Jeremiah are, by preference, types of the true patriot. The New Testament shows us the God-Man, born of a poor Israelite woman, totally dedicated to his people and restricting his direct activity to them. He chose his Apostles from Israel alone and sent them to Israel alone—only right at the end are they sent on a mission to other nations (Matt 10:5 ff; 26:18; John 10:8). In this respect the disciples of Jesus followed his example, as also did St.

1. 1936, pp. 65–74.
2. The natural revelation of God which comes from the Logos and enlightens and directs those peoples who are not the object of God's supernatural revelation.

Paul, Apostle to the Gentiles, who in the first eleven chapters of his Epistle to the Romans gives expression to the deep and tender attachment which he had to his own people. Faithful to the Lord's command to the Twelve, he preached the Gospel first to Jews and turned to the Gentiles only when the Jews rejected him.[3] Even then he did not deny the preeminent role which the Jews had in the work of salvation.[4] Convert Gentiles are described by Paul as "fellow heirs, members of the same body and partakers of the promise in Christ Jesus" (Eph 3:6) and by Peter as "a chosen race, a holy nation, God's own people" (1 Pet 2:9–10). These Gentiles were all indistinctly given the name "Greeks"; the national name of the culturally most important people at that time was taken as a synonym for "Gentile." This was correct insofar as the Greeks did really form the advance guard of the Gentiles converted to Christianity or, to use another metaphor, constituted the "new dough" from which was kneaded a new Gentile world, Greek in culture and Christian, forming the "new" or the "third race."[5]

Harnack, too, came eventually to acknowledge this. He wrote: "From the point of view of language Christianity became a Greek movement and remained so almost to the end of the second century. Even in the centuries which followed, in spite of all the struggles against Hellenism, Greek Christianity gave support to the Greek spirit in many different regions of the East among peoples of different tongues, and in so doing continued the work of Alexander the Great" —with the exception of the Syrians, Copts, Armenians, and Goths "whom the Chrisitan Greeks were not able to hellenize." Harnack, however, did not ascribe this last merely to a loss of strength on the part of Hellenism; there also entered into play the weakening of Christianity and the severe losses which it sustained in the following centuries. In fact he goes on: "if these peoples had been hellenized with the help of the Church the course of history would have been different and Islam would probably have been limited to the Arab world."[6]

The Christians of the first age were not only convinced that they formed a *"novum genus"*; they were also a *"nova civitas"* as we see in

---

3. Acts 13:5 ff; 14:1 ff; 16:13 ff; 17:2 ff.
4. Rom 2:10, 17 ff; 3:1 ff; 9:1 ff; 10:1 ff; 11:1 ff.
5. See Eph 2:11 ff; Barnabas 5:7; 9:5; Ignatius, *Eph* 19:20; Aristides, *Apol.* 2; Justin, *Dial.* 119; *Diognetus* 5; Clement Alex., *Strom.* III, 10, 70; Eusebius, *Hist. Eccl.* I, 4.
6. A. Harnack, *Mission und Ausbreitung des Christentums in den ersten drei Jahrhunderten,* II, pp. 266–267.

the Acts of the Apostles. Moreover, they were convinced that they possessed a "new philosophy" and that the Church was the κόσμος τοῦ κόσμου ("the world of [within] the world") in the phrase coined by Origen.[7]

As was to be expected, differences of nationality in the Roman and later in the Byzantine world became less important or were even deleted under the influence of this Christian and Greco-Roman cosmopolitan way of thinking. There predominated above all the consciousness of belonging as citizens in the real sense of the word to a "new nation" (καινῆς πολιτείας).

At all events, the Church in the Greek Christian East had from ancient times given importance to the national character of the peoples who belonged to her in following the freedom-loving tradition which is proper to Christian and Greek. She not only permitted the use of the vernacular but was also the means of strengthening it through the liturgy and the translation of the Bible into Syriac, Coptic, Ethiopian, Gothic, Armenian, Arabic, and the Slavic languages. This was already taking place in the second century, while in the West, as is well known, Latin was prescribed as the only ecclesiastical language both for liturgy and the reading of the Scriptures. It is once again Harnack who stresses the fact that "the Greek Church, even to the detriment of its own national advancement, prepared the ground for national literatures among those peoples who previously had no literature or even no writings of their own at all. All this was set in motion by the reading of the Bible which was promoted by the Greeks."[8]

On the other hand, however, this molding of a national consciousness, leading at times to a sense of nationalism, brought several of these peoples to accept the Monophysite heresy of the Byzantine statechurch. In reaction to this, and also as a consequence of the rebirth of classical studies in Byzantium (already begun under the Macedonian dynasty, 867–1057), there was a reawakening of Greek national consciousness among the Byzantines. We can see this already in the works of Photius under the Commene dynasty (1081–1185), and it finally grew to great strength at the time of the Palaeologi. It is noteworthy that the last emperor of this dynasty, although he bore the title of Roman Emperor, addressed Constantinople as "the joy of all Hellenes" (χαρὰ πάντων τῶν Ἑλλήνων) on the tragic night during which the

7. In John 6:38.
8. "Über den privaten Gebrauch der Heiligen Schriften in der alten Kirche," in *Beiträge zur Einleitung in das Neue Testament*, V, p. 60.

famous city fell to the Turks. He bequeathed this title as a precious national and political inheritance to those Byzantine peoples who had fallen under the alien yoke. And in fact the Greek-speaking and Greek-thinking population of the city fallen under the Turkish yoke maintained not only the Orthodox faith but also its Greek national consciousness with the help of the liturgy and the unwearying service of the Church's priests and monks. It also preserved unshaken the hope of a political restoration. This consciousness and hope were the fundamental prerequisites for the liberation of the Greek nation in the nineteenth century.

The Orthodox Church also played a somewhat parallel role in Russia when Russian Christians were enslaved in the thirteenth century. The same occurred in Rumania, Serbia, and Bulgaria, which remained for several centuries under Turkish rule.

We do not wish to dispute the fact that within the Orthodox Church the local Churches have been associated with the nations in which they were established more closely than in the other great Churches. But we take leave to doubt that there are many other nations whose Churches have rendered them so great a service as the Orthodox Church has to hers. I am thinking not only of achievements in the religious field but also of those which are cultural and economic, which concern the existence of each nation as such.[9] It is absolutely necessary for the harmonious and successful cooperation of a national church with a nation that the latter should give a positive evaluation to what the Church does for it and that, moreover, it should give to the Church a place in its life as a nation which is analogous to the soul in relation to the human organism. This is a great truth which is often overlooked or misunderstood, and this misunderstanding has been the occasion of great harm and has given rise to the reproach continually made against the Orthodox Church that it has become the slave of a gross form of nationalism or even chauvinism.[10]

We conclude this chapter with one or two important observations:

1. This reproach of chauvinism has been often made against the Ecumenical Patriarchate and the Greek-speaking Orthodox Church in general. In rebuttal of this we have the historical record of the undivided Church of the first eight centuries. To testify to the broad approach of the Greek Church and its emphasis on the spiritual in its

9. A. Müller-Armack, *Religion und Wirtschaft*, 1959, pp. 328–370.
10. A. Harnack, *Wesen des Christentums, Lehrbuch der Dogmengeschichte*, II (5th ed.), pp. 43 ff.

relation to the ancient national churches of the East we have not only the examples adduced by Harnack;[11] the services rendered by Greek missionaries in the cultural field to the Slavic churches founded by them should also be mentioned. It is well known that these peoples owe not only their alphabet and system of writing but also the translation of the Bible and the liturgy—and with that the beginnings of their own national literatures—to these Greek missionaries, among whom we should mention Methodius, Cyril, and Maximus the Greek in particular. Even in later times the history of Russia and the Balkan nations has much to say on the valuable contribution of the Ecumenical Patriarchate, and not least for the preservation of the distinct national character of these peoples; how else are we to understand the fact that the title "Mother Church" (Μήτηρ 'Εκκλησία) used of the Ecumenical Patriarchate has passed into common usage in these national churches. All of this is stated and acknowledged by the leading historians of the Slavic peoples and the Rumanians, and, in fact, from Professor Zankow at Herzeg Novi the author first learned of what these historians have to say after he delivered his paper entitled "State, Nation, Church: An Orthodox Viewpoint."[12]

2. The Orthodox Church condemned this outright kind of nationalism at a local council held at Constantinople in 1872.

3. The Orthodox Church is always prepared to acknowledge the particular contribution which each nation, according to the specific gifts which it has been given, has made in the furtherance of Gospel and Church.

BIBLIOGRAPHY

S. ZANKOW, "Kirche und Nation in Orthodoxen Osten," in *Die Kirche und das Staatsproblem in der Gegenwart* (a research paper in connection with the Ecumenical Council for Practical Christianity, 1934); P. BRATSIOTIS, "Staat, Nation, Kirche," in *Internationale Kirchliche Zeitschrift,* Bern, 1936, pp. 65–75.

11. See above pp. 71–72.
12. See above pp. 69–70.

ORTHODOX CHURCH AND STATE

WITH REGARD to the relation between the Orthodox Church and the state, one could say that the basic principles are identical with those we have laid down above on the situation of the Church vis-à-vis the world and the nation, for the state too is an element or aspect of the world in which the Church has to act as the soul does with regard to the human organism. The method which the Orthodox Church uses in normal circumstances to regulate its relations with the state goes by the name of "symphonia," which literally means accord, consonance. It implies that the Church is free in respect of its own internal and spiritual affairs and that the competence of the state is limited to external and secular matters. But since "the whole world is in the power of the evil one" (1 John 5:19), a perfect "symphonia" remains an unattainable ideal. There is always the danger that the balance will somehow be lost. As the history of the Byzantine Church, the Russian Church under the czars, and the Balkan Churches shows, there are many lapses from the ideal and much friction between the two. At any rate, the history of the Orthodox Church provides no example of political interference of the Church in state affairs—with the exception of the special privileges granted to the Church under Turkish domination. This in fact is explicitly forbidden by the canons of the Orthodox Church. There are, on the other hand, plenty of examples of abuse of power by the state and even regular persecutions which can compare with those of the first centuries of Church history, as the iconoclast period and the Turkish domination in particular.

Soon after the emancipation of the Church of Greece from the Ecumenical Patriarchate in 1852, which was a result of the changed political scene resulting from the liberation of Greece from the Turks, the system of Church-state relations elaborated by the well-known Bavarian lawyer G. L. Maurer[1] in accordance with foreign (i.e., Bavarian and Russian) models was officially introduced. This system was in some respects the opposite of the constitution of the Greek Church in 1844. The first two articles of the new constitution

1. Maurer was a member of the regency council set up during the minority of King Otto I (1833–1834).

dealt with the Orthodox Church as representative of the official state religion, her spiritual bond with the other Orthodox Churches, her independence, and her right to administer her own affairs on the basis of her sacred canons. These two articles are still in force today. At the same time the state retained the right under this system not only to decide legislation even in affairs belonging to ecclesiastical administration but even to elect a bishop from the three candidates put forward by the Holy Synod. This provision was in force until twenty-four years ago, but from the latter part of 1923 the whole system began to be modified in favor of Church autonomy, though unfortunately the rights of priests and laity, sanctioned by the Bible and Church history, were not sufficiently taken into account. Five years ago a mixed commission of bishops and university professors was established according to law with the task of drawing up a new constitution for the Church of Greece. At the time of writing, this constitution has not yet been officially sanctioned. Despite the agelong luster of the Orthodox tradition a just canonical regulation of the relations between Church and state is not easy even in Greece, for the secularist spirit becomes more widespread as time goes on. It is necessary nonetheless that the many privileges of priests and laity in church administration should receive their due recognition as a counterbalance to the strongly asserted power of the hierarchy. After all, according to Scripture and the sacred canons, the difference between bishop and priest is not so great—οὐ πολὺ τὸ μέσον ("The distance is not so great"), says St. John Chrysostom—and the laity is the body of the Church.

BIBLIOGRAPHY

CHR. ANDROUTSOS, *Church and State* (in Greek), 1918; H. ALIVISATOS, "Das kanonische Recht der Orthodoxen Kirche," in *Ekklesia,* ed. F. SIEGMUND SCHULTZE, 1939; H. KOTSONIS, "Die Stellung der Laien in der Orthodoxen Kirche," in *Orthodoxe Kirche in griechischer Sicht,* II, 1960, pp. 93–115; P. POULITSAS, "Die Beziehungen zwischen Staat und Kirche in Griechenland," *ibid.,* II, 1960, pp. 38–48.

BASIC PRINCIPLES AND ESSENTIAL CHARACTERISTICS OF ORTHODOXY

HAVING BRIEFLY OUTLINED, without any pretensions to completeness, a confessional point of view on the history of the Orthodox Church and the content of its faith, I would like now to set out and summarize with equal brevity the basic principles and essential characteristics of this Church and its position vis-à-vis the other Churches. In the paper which I read at the First Congress for Orthodox Theology held in Athens in 1936[1] I gave pride of place to a loyal adhesion to the sacred tradition inherited from the ancient Church before the division as the basic principle and main criterion of Orthodox continuity. The Orthodox Church is essentially a church built on tradition, for her tradition is of greater value than anything else. Others may blame us for this, but for us it is a subject for legitimate pride. Loyalty to ancient and even apostolic tradition is not simply attachment to the past for its own sake or to some external criterion of authority; above all, it is not torpidity as Harnack and other Protestant, and even some Roman Catholic, theologians have supposed. The latter, of course, give great importance to tradition but accept at the same time the principle of the so-called development of doctrine. In our Church, tradition is the second source of belief but, as we have seen,[2] is to be taken together with the first source, which is holy Scripture. So we draw the unavoidable conclusion that just as the true meaning of Scripture must not be distorted, so tradition must remain unchanged.

At the same time, tradition in the Orthodox Church is not, as some Christians of other confessions believe, something static. We con-

1. Both the theme of the congress and my own paper bore the same title as this chapter. See H. Alivisatos, *Procès-Verbaux du I Congrès de Théologie Orthodoxe à Athènes*, 1938.
2. See above pp. 25 ff.

ceive it as dynamic. Loyalty to tradition is a living bond with the fullness of the centuries-long experience of the Church. Tradition is in reality a means of contact with the Word of God, the source from which eternal life springs (John 4:14). This was how it was seen in the ancient Church before the division.

Another basic principle of Orthodoxy is a finely balanced association of *authority* and *freedom*,[3] once again in imitation of the ancient Church. With regard to doctrine a further basic characteristic which should be recognized is the emphasis laid on the *Incarnation of the Logos* and especially the *divinity of Christ*, to which corresponds the *theosis of man*,[4] a correspondence which has been a commonplace of Orthodox theology since the time of Irenaeus and Athanasius, chiefly due to the great influence of the writings of these two Fathers of the Church.

This will help to clarify the point I made earlier, that the greatest and most exalted feast, the feast of feasts in the Orthodox Church, is Easter. For Christ our God, through his resurrection "has transferred us from death to life and from earth to heaven, and by his passion has clothed corruptible nature with incorruption."[5]

Yet another essential character of the Orthodox Church consists in the fact that she directs her gaze toward eternity and the life to come, whence her strong insistence on *the transitory nature of created things. The expectation of the last things* has always been a living reality to her. It is this note which, together with the emphasis on the divinization of man in Christ,[6] gives a strong ascetical and mystical coloring to her piety. Yet this undeniable fact does not justify the idea entertained by some Christians of other confessions, whether theologians or not, that the Orthodox Church is characterized by a quietistic indifference to human knowledge, culture, or in fact anything human at all. Much less can the objection be maintained that this peculiar characteristic of the Orthodox Church is the chief reason why she shows no evidence of any real social activity (as proposed by Harnack, Kattenbusch, K. Beth, Steffes, Müller-Armack, and others). All of this

3. In 1931 I wrote a small study on this theme entitled *Authority and Freedom in Orthodox Theology* (in Greek).

4. See above pp. 38 f.

5. From the canon of St. John Damascene in the *Orthros* of the Orthodox Easter liturgy.

6. See "Die Lehre der Orthodoxen Kirche über die Theosis des Menschen," in *Mededelingen van de Koninklijke Vlaamse Akademie,* Klasse der Letteren, XXIII, 1961, No. 1.

betrays at the very least a misrepresentation of the facts, if not ignorance, of the history of the Orthodox Church. The otherworldly character of the Eastern Church, the looking to eternity and the world to come, was already present in the ancient Church and among the early Christians. Suffice it to indicate one or two texts from the New Testament and early Christian literature. We have the words of the Lord: "Do not lay up for yourselves treasures on earth, where moth and rust consume and where thieves break in and steal" (Matt 6:19 ff), the words of St. Paul: "our commonwealth is in heaven" (Phil 3:20), and finally the text we have already quoted from the Epistle to Diognetus: "Christians dwell in their own fatherlands but as wayfarers; they take part in everything but only as citizens; and they endure everything as strangers" (5:5). That *eschatological thinking* was a live issue in the early Church hardly needs to be proved.

The *ascetical and mystical* element which runs through early Christianity and the history of the early Church and which is deeply rooted in the New Testament is intimately connected with this. We read in Matthew 19:12: "For there are eunuchs who have been so from birth, and there are eunuchs who have been made eunuchs by men, and there are eunuchs who have made themselves eunuchs for the sake of the kingdom of heaven," and in St. Paul, "I pommel my body and subdue it, lest after preaching to others I myself should be disqualified" (1 Cor 9:27). We could also refer to the superiority of the unmarried state to marriage in St. Paul (1 Cor 7:1ff), the aversion of the early Church to second marriages, and the practice of fasting which was introduced very early in imitation of Christ.[7] Even Harnack had to admit that the rigorist element in Christianity goes back to the second century.[8]

Finally, as regards *the mystical element* which Orthodoxy has in common with the early Church, suffice it to refer to what we find in Paul's letter to the Philippians.[9] We should further note before passing on that this ascetic and mystical element did not prevent the early Church from taking a keen interest in social questions and showing herself open to culture and the pursuit of knowledge.[10] Neither has

7. Matt. 4:2 ff; 17:21; Acts 14:23; 1 Cor 7:5; 2 Cor 6:6.

8. *Das Wesen des Christentums*, p. 133.

9. For the New Testament as a whole see G. A. Deissmann, *Paul*, New York, 1957; E. Weber, *Eschatologie und Mystik im Neuen Testament*, 1930.

10. Uhlhorn, *Die christliche Liebestätigkeit in der alten Kirche*, 1882; A. Harnack, *The Mission and Expansion of Christianity in the First Three Centuries*, 1908; L. Koukoules, *Leben und Kultur der Byzantiner*, II, 1948 (in Greek), pp. 64–178.

it prevented the Orthodox Church from performing precious services in the social, cultural, and political sphere to those peoples who belong to her. While we do not deny the fact that the Orthodox Church cannot emulate either the Roman Catholic or the Protestant Churches in external missionary work or internal social activity, we must state that the reasons for this are historical and do not arise from the nature of Orthodoxy itself. There is no reason, therefore, why with time they should not be overcome.

The Orthodox Church is also characterized by its recognition of *the rights that belong to the laity*. This is true not only in church administration but also in liturgy and teaching, that is, in the whole range of church life. At the same time she acknowledges the superior position of the clergy—above all that of the bishops—in the body of the Church and maintains the hierarchical (not hierocratic!) character which the Church assumed in the first centuries of her history. When, as it sometimes happens, the rights of the laity have not been or are not respected in practice, this must be seen as a falling away from the true spirit of Orthodoxy.

A basic distinguishing mark of the Orthodox Church is also the system of *governing by synod*. This is practiced both in the individual autocephalous member Churches and in the direction of the Church as a whole. As is well known, Orthodoxy took over this system of governing from the ancient Church; it is a heritage which she must not on any account abandon.

We should mention finally that the Orthodox Church *renounces the use of political power*. In this respect our Church acts in accordance with the words of the Lord: "Render therefore to Caesar the things that are Caesar's, and to God the things that are God's" (Matt 22:21) and "My kingdom is not of this world" (John 18:36).

ORTHODOX CHURCH AND THE OTHER MAIN CHRISTIAN BODIES

PROTESTANT THEOLOGIANS such as N. Söderblom and F. Heiler have attempted to summarize the main characteristics of each of the three great Christian bodies by means of a biblical catchword. The Roman Catholic Church is Petrine, the Protestant Pauline, and the Orthodox Johannine. Such an attempt, however, is bound to be one-sided and, in Orthodox eyes at least, does not correspond with the facts. The Orthodox Church is convinced that she has remained faithful to the character impressed on the Church by *all* the Apostles and that her children not only believe in the *one, holy, catholic, and apostolic Church* but also belong to her.

As for how our Church stands in relation to the others, most Orthodox would take the view that their form of Christian faith has a position somewhere between Roman Catholicism and Protestantism, but one much nearer to the former than the latter. This last view would, however, be disputed by many enthusiasts for ecumenism and—at least up to recent times—by those theologians who were not favorable to Roman Catholicism.[1] Some would even take the opposite view. This, however, is rejected—and in my view correctly—by some prominent Protestant theologians. An example would be F. Heiler, who holds the view that "this habit of contrasting the Orthodox Church and Rome rests, on the one hand, on an inexact knowledge of the doctrine and practice of the Roman Church and, on the other, on a falsely 'modern view of Orthodoxy."[2] Among the Protestant Churches those which approach nearest to Orthodoxy are first of all the Lutherans with their

1. The view that the Orthodox Church has a position somewhere between Roman Catholicism and Protestantism is accepted not only by Orthodox theologians but by many Catholics and Protestants.
2. F. Heiler, *Urkirche und Ostkirche,* p. 561.

well-defined confession of faith (the *Confessio Augustana,* the Apologia, and the Articles of Smalkald) and the Anglican High Church. The basic difference between the Roman Catholic and Orthodox Churches is, according to our view, the Roman exaggeration of authority invested in the person of the pope, to whom absolute primacy of jurisdiction and infallibility are ascribed. The basic difference between us and Protestants is their exaggeration of liberty to the detriment of the authority of both Church and Scripture.

Despite all these differences and contrasts we should not, however, lose sight of our common belief in the Bible as the Word of God, in the trinitarian dogma, in the one, holy, catholic, and apostolic Church, in the one baptism for the remission of sins, the resurrection of the dead, and the life to come. These, after all, are the main articles of the Apostles' Creed and that established at the councils of Nicaea and Constantinople. In addition to this, the Orthodox accept that each of the great Churches of the West has its own good characteristics and has great achievements to its credit, including the dissemination and interpretation of Scripture, the defense and spread of Christianity, the encouragement of theology, the creation of a Christian culture, raising the standard of living, care for the poor, the sick, and those who have suffered injustice and, indeed, for every class of people.

All of these accomplishments have been clearly acknowledged by Greek theologians, even in the days when the walls of division between the Churches were very high and little thought was given to the question of Church unity. Similarly, the Western Churches have repeatedly acknowledged the value of the Orthodox Church and its achievements. This is true not only of Protestants from the time of Melanchthon down to K. Holl, F. Heiler, and others but also of popes as outstanding as Pius XI and John XXIII. In an address delivered to the Union of Catholic Universities Pius XI said: "The praiseworthy Eastern Christian Churches have preserved a sanctity of such a high standard that it deserves the highest recognition and honor," and to close this chapter I quote an observation of F. Heiler occasioned by this statement of Pope Pius. He remarks: "This admiration which the Pope professes for the Eastern Church was naturally tempered with some reserve for dogmatic and juridical reasons, but the same admiration found expression in the exclamation of a simple Italian girl of the Third Order of St. Francis who became familiar with Orthodox liturgy in the Uniate abbey of Grottaferrata in Rome: 'O blessed Oriental Church!' "[3]

3. *Ibid.,* p. 567.

THE RELATION BETWEEN CHURCH AND THEOLOGY IN ORTHODOXY

THE ORTHODOX CHURCH is in harmonious relationship with theology since it is the science proper to her, for which she provides both meaning and content. This does not at all imply that these good relations are established at the price of the scientific character of theology on the one hand or its confessional nature on the other. The fact that Orthodox theology has a confessional character does not prevent it from being scientific. To be scientific, theology does not have to be absolutely without presuppositions of any kind, as it was supposed during the nineteenth century when positivism held sway. Nor does it require an unrestricted freedom of enquiry such as to dissolve those internal and external bonds by which the human soul lives. The essence of scientific theology lies in its sincere and untiring search for the truth, not in its freedom from presuppositions, and, in fact, these presuppositions are not absent in Orthodox theology. It is significant that in Greece professors of theology are appointed by the state after they are proposed by the university faculties without any approval by the Sacred Synod, yet the Orthodox clergy receive their scientific theological formation in these same universities.

Following the tradition of the ancient Church, the Orthodox Church always respects the freedom of theologians, as well as of those engaged in other sciences, provided, of course, that they remain within the limits of their own discipline and do not openly attack the Church.

When speaking of the various *schools of thought* in modern Orthodox theology, we have to bear in mind that the Orthodox Church is built on tradition and that she has found her own way of combining liberty and authority. This implies that Orthodox theology has also succeeded in combining freedom of research with respect for the claims of faith and the tradition which the Church preserves and holds in high honor. It is averse both to an ultraconservative stance and to modernistic trends. To be sure, such tendencies have appeared from time to time in the history of the Orthodox Church, but they have never found any permanent support. There is the same basic contradiction between ultraconservatism and theological science as there is between the Church and modernism.

We should say a brief word about the more important *centers of Orthodox theological study*. In Russia material conditions favored a development in theological study. The brothers Joannikios and Sphronios Lichoudae, who came from Greece, founded a Greco-Slavic theological academy in Moscow as early as 1687. Soon afterwards Kiev achieved preeminence in scientific study, including theology, under Peter the Great. After the founding of the Theological Academy of Kiev in the eighteenth century similar academies were established in St. Petersburg, Moscow, and Kazan. These centers of learning, founded and maintained by the Church, dedicated themselves with great enthusiasm to the study of theology. Bishops, the higher clergy, and many of the laity received their education there. Only two of these academies still exist in Russia, those in Moscow and Leningrad.

The Ecumenical Patriarchate founded the academies of Constantinople, Athos, Patmos, Bucharest, and Iasi. Many well-known Greeks studied in the theological faculty of the Ionian Academy of Corfu founded in 1824. The University of Athens, which was established by King Otto on German lines in 1837, five years after the founding of the Greek state, had its own theological faculty from the very beginning, whereas a theological faculty was formed in the University of Thessalonica only in 1942. As early as 1843 the Ecumenical Patriarchate had founded a theological college on the island of Chalcos near Constantinople for the training of its clergy, and it was there too that the prospective bishops of the other ancient patriarchates, and also those of Rumania, Bulgaria, and sometimes Serbia, received their education. In 1845 a theological college was established in the Monastery of the Holy Cross belonging to the Patriarchate of Jerusalem, the last rector of which was Chrysostom Papadopoulos, later professor at the University of Athens and archbishop of the same city (✝ 1938). Until 1920 the Orthodox clergy of Serbia were formed in the theological college of Karlowitz, thereafter at the theological faculty of the University of Belgrade, and sometimes at the University of Athens, as was the case with Patriarch Gabriel, who died in 1848.

Under the present regime the theological faculty of Belgrade has been turned into an ecclesiastical seminary under the jurisdiction of the Serbian Patriarchate. In Rumania there were theological faculties at the universities of Bucharest, Sibiu, and Tschernovic, in spite of which many Rumanian professors and bishops were educated in Athens, as, for example, the present metropolitan of Iasi, Justin Moysescu. At the present time the Rumanian Patriarchate has two theological institutes in Bucharest and Sibiu. As a rule, the Bulgarian clergy receives its theological formation in the theological faculty of the University of Sophia, but some go to Russia, Rumania, and Greece.

I should refer, finally, to the Pan-Orthodox theological congress of 1936 which came about through the initiative of the theological faculty of the University of Athens under the presidency of Professor Alivisatos. This was a welcome sign of the living reality of theological studies within the Church and the effect which they have on the spiritual lives of the Orthodox peoples. The acts of this congress were published in a handsome volume in 1939. Noteworthy also were the Panhellenic theological congresses held in Athens during the last few decades, the first in 1930, followed by others in 1951 and 1963.

BIBLIOGRAPHY

D. BALANOS, "Geschichte der griechischen kirchlichen Literatur," in *Ekklesia*, X, pp. 36–54; P. BRATSIOTIS, *Autorität und Freiheit in der Orthodoxen Theologie*, 1931; *Die griechische Theologie in den letzen fünfzig Jahren*, 1948.

RELIGIOUS MOVEMENTS IN THE ORTHODOX CHURCH

THE ORTHODOX PEOPLES are distinguished by a deep piety and religious sense which is connected with their national character. This innate religiosity has been strengthened by the following factors: a long tradition, especially in the case of the Greeks, who are the oldest of the Orthodox nations; a strong link between the Orthodox nations and the Church to which they owe their survival during difficult times of persecution; the influence of the liturgy, so splendidly rich in religious inspiration and instruction.

An external indication of this piety can be found in the numerous churches which one finds everywhere in Orthodox countries, especially in Greece. We should add, however, that the lack of adequate religious instruction, especially during the Turkish domination, was responsible for the growth of superstition and some diminution of the true spirit of the Gospel, which is also that of the Orthodox Church. Yet, despite this, the Orthodox peoples have diligently preserved their faith and produced numerous saints and martyrs. At the time of the Enlightenment and the various attacks upon Christianity which sprang from it, the national Orthodox Churches pitted their traditional faith and way of life against the dangerous philosophies coming from both West and East. They had before them the example of devoted scholars reared among the subjected nations and Orthodox monasticism nourished from the fountainhead of monasticism at Mount Athos. A spiritual movement which began at Mount Athos at the end of the eighteenth century and which was taken up and developed in all the Orthodox countries led to very significant results. I do not, however, propose to follow this subject any further with respect to the other Orthodox countries since I am too little acquainted with them, but will limit myself to some important factors in Greek church history of recent years.[1]

1. See P. Bratsiotis, "Die geistigen Bewegungen und religiosen Stromungen in der Orthodoxen Kirche Griechenlands," in *Die Orthodoxe Kirche in griechischer Sicht,* II, pp. 49 ff.

In the last century the national church of Greece strongly resisted some dangerous ideas and practices coming from the West. At the same time as the liberation of the first part of Greece in 1829 there began an ascetical and mystical movement of renewal which was to develop in the course of time and produce very salutary results. At the beginning it was carried forward enthusiastically by the monks Christopher Papoulakis and Cosmas Flamiatos, but it was really the work of Apostolos Makrakis († 1905), an almost entirely self-taught philosopher and theologian from the Island of Siphnos. From his school came, among others, the future Archimandrate Eusebios Mathopoulos,[2] who, together with his pupils Panagis Trembelas (later professor of theology), Dionysios Pharasoulis, and Demetrios Panagiotopoulos, founded in 1907 the society of theologians called *Zoe* (Life). It was Father Eusebios' purpose to form in the members of his society a truly Christian personality and to make them dynamic members of the Orthodox Church. He strove with clergy and laity to bring about a rebirth of Christianity in the Greek people. For over half a century this society provided great support for the national church. In Greece, Cyprus, and even further afield it spread the Gospel by the written and spoken word, called the people to repentance, met their needs in the confessional, set up Sunday schools, founded a liturgical movement, and organized different kinds of groups and associations. This movement has therefore contributed greatly to renewal in the Church. Since the last war it has also dedicated itself to the sick and the poor. But after fifty years of meritorious activity God permitted that the brotherhood should divide and each half go its own way. One part, made up of most of the clerics and those of Father Eusebios' disciples and co-workers who were still alive, founded the confraternity called *Soter* (The Savior), while the other, composed of most of the younger members, kept the name and with it the assets of the original organization. In the seven years since its establishment the new confraternity *Soter* has made great progress and has contributed to spreading the Word of God even further afield among the people.

This, however, is not the only movement of spiritual renewal in the Greek Church. After those just mentioned, the most significant of these is one founded by Father Mark Tsaktanis, the married priest, and led by his brother-in-law Father Angelos Nissiotis. It is called the "Orthodox Union" and is for men, women, students, and young peo-

2. S. Papakostas. *Eusebios Mathopoulos,* 1930 (English trans. 1939).

ple. *Apostolike Diakonia* (Apostolic Service) was founded by the Holy Synod of the Church of Greece. In a manner similar to that of private movements, it seeks new ways of presenting the faith and instructs the faithful—the young in particular—by means of sermons, Sunday schools, and religious writing. *Apostolike Diakonia,* with its headquarters in the monastery of Petraki, established a residence for students of theology, a center for deaconesses, and the student hostel of St. Barbara with the material assistance of the World Council of Churches. It is also in the process of editing the Greek Church Fathers in its own publishing house. So far about forty volumes have appeared.

I should also mention briefly the work of renewal being carried out by the well-known republic of monasteries on Mount Athos. Here Russian, Serbian, and Bulgarian monks, together with some living in a Rumanian *Skete,*[3] are engaged in translating the famous ascetical collection *Philokalia*[4] into their respective languages and disseminating it throughout Russia and the Balkans. This has had very beneficial results.[5]

3. A kind of small monastery.
4. A collection of writings of Greek mystics.
5. See F. Heiler, *Urkirche und Ostkirche,* 1937, pp. 408 ff; article in *Istina,* 1958, pp. 295–328, 443–474.

ORTHODOX CHURCH AND ECUMENICAL MOVEMENT

THE ENCYCLICAL "To All the Churches of Christ" which the Ecumenical Patriarchate sent in 1920 to the other Churches gave a great impulse to the ecumenical movement which came into the open after the First World War. In this encyclical the suggestion was made to form a "league of churches" corresponding to the League of Nations founded at that time in Geneva. This society was to have the purpose of promoting cooperation in practical matters among the Churches. The first World Conference of Churches met in Stockholm in 1925 under the title "For Life and Work." In spite of the impatient zeal of many people engaged in the ecumenical movement, the Ecumenical Patriarchate adhered to this line of practical cooperation as the encyclical of 1951 addressed to all the Orthodox Churches shows. In the last few years, however, the World Council of Churches has been trying to widen the area of cooperation and is seeking for compromise formulae in order to manifest more concretely the unity of the Church. In meetings held just a few years ago in Montreal and Rochester the suggestion was made to broaden the concept of "church." In general, people today prefer to speak of unity and unification in Christ rather than of the unity of the Churches, and of the need for an ecumenical consciousness rather than of the need to remove the ecclesiological differences between the Churches.

Our efforts today are directed to working out an ecumenical theology. Rather than try to change people's ways of thinking, we prefer to work out new practical methods of putting aside the obstacle of dogmatic differences between the Churches. All the effort is directed to leading back the divided Churches to the basic form and structure of the ancient undivided Church by seeking new ways of understanding the division. Most Protestant Churches which belong to the World Council of Churches are represented at meetings by theologians who are not tied to the dogmatic tradition of their own Churches but more often than not merely voice their own views. When, however, one

91

considers the different ways of thinking and dogmatic presuppositions, the different views about Scripture and ecclesiological problems of the individual members of the World Council, even to discuss possible ways of practical cooperation seems no light task.

On the credit side, the largest of today's Churches, namely, the Roman Catholic communion, is showing an increasing interest in the World Council of Churches. Despite its own ecumenical or catholic character, however, it has so far not taken any official part in the World Council despite repeated invitations to do so.[1] The long absence of the Roman Catholic Church from this organization, the encyclical *Mortalium animos,* and a *monitum* of the Holy Office on the subject[2] provide food for thought for Orthodox Christians today. One can therefore imagine the embarrassment in which the representatives of the Orthodox Church at the world conference on "Faith and Order" (Lausanne, 1927) found themselves when they felt obliged to make a special statement on their own position. It is noteworthy that the initiative for this necessary measure came from the Athenian delegation.

An apparently more optimistic attitude to our Protestant brethren on the part of the Greek Orthodox Church could give the false impression that this Church regards itself as just one among many Churches. We dare not suppose that the Roman Catholic Church, if some day it sends representatives to an ecumenical meeting of this kind, would be prepared to make such a "gesture of courtesy."

The Orthodox who took part in the world conference "Faith and Order" held in Edinburgh in 1937 followed the example of the Orthodox delegation at Lausanne. Out of courtesy the Orthodox delegation was almost led to limit its participation to some dogmatic formulations in the acts of the conference, but eventually the special situation of the Orthodox Church and the attitude of the Orthodox delegation at Lausanne were taken into account, and a new declaration on the part of the Orthodox Church was read at the end of the plenary session. I had the honor to belong to the Greek delegation at this conference and was able to have a direct and personal experience of the ecumenical movement and to form some idea of what the future attitude of the Orthodox Church might be. In a full report made for the Holy Synod, which was published in *Ekklesia,*[3] I emphasized among other

1. I feel obliged to draw attention to one such open invitation recorded in the official organ of the Church of Greece, *Ekklesia,* 1947, Vols. 33–34, published in French in *Irenikon,* 1948, Vol. 1.

2. See P. Bratsiotis, in *Ekklesia,* 1950, Nos. 18 and 19, pp. 302 ff.

3. 1938, Vols. 10–11.

things that, from the Orthodox side, the ecumenical movement ought to follow the blueprint laid down in the above-mentioned encyclical letter of the Ecumenical Patriarchate. This stated that cooperation among the Churches on the level of practical Christianity must be promoted and a common front formed against anti-Christian movements in the modern world. Above all, the words of Jesus, "that all may be one," must be taken as the basis for unity in faith. This was in agreement with Professor C. Androutsos, the great Greek dogmatic theologian and philosopher.[4]

This conviction of mine was strengthened by what I experienced at the plenary gathering at the World Conference of Churches at Amsterdam which came together in August, 1948, after preparatory work going back as far as 1937.

At this meeting the World Council of Churches was established and its constitution drawn up. The Orthodox Church also took part in this critically important conference, but only through representatives of the Ecumenical Patriarchate, the Church of Greece (twelve representatives, among them four metropolitans), the Church of Cyprus, and the Russian diaspora. Archbishop Germanos of Thyatira was at the head of the Orthodox delegation.

The members of the Greek delegation were poorly impressed right at the start of the proceedings when the representatives of the different Churches were received in the Amsterdam cathedral. This was carried out, not according to the historical precedence of the divided Churches, but in alphabetical order.

Unacceptable also from the Orthodox viewpoint was the mixing together of the two organizations "Life and Work" and "Faith and Order." This was not in keeping with the spirit of the 1920 encyclical of the Ecumenical Patriarchate and was therefore strenuously resisted by most of the Orthodox present. What, however, upset the Orthodox delegation most was the fact that faith in Christ as God and redeemer was made the basis of the World Council of Churches rather than faith in the blessed Trinity as the Orthodox, together with Old Catholics, Lutherans, and many Anglicans, had hoped.

For the majority of the orthodox delegation a critical point was reached when the special declaration drawn up by them at Lausanne and Edinburgh in keeping with Orthodox tradition was set aside, and in its place a rather colorless address of Archbishop Germanos of

4. See his *Symbolik*, 1930², pp. 414 f.

Thyatira was read in the last plenary session.[5]

When after the return of the Orthodox delegation its report was published, together with a memorandum which I drew up for the Holy Synod, a storm of indignation broke out in the religious press and in fact throughout the whole of the Greek Church. There were those who thought that despite all our vigilance and spirit of independence in Church matters, Orthodoxy was being gradually weakened in the pervasively Protestant milieu of these meetings. The tireless and courageous leader of this reaction was Irenaeus, metropolitan of Samos (1963), certainly the most able philosopher and theologian among the Greek bishops.[6]

The result of this reaction became apparent in 1952 when the Greek Church took no part in the "Faith and Order" world conference of Churches held in Lund, and the Holy Synod expressed its disapproval of any further participation of Orthodox bishops in these ecumenical meetings. Going a step further, the Orthodox delegation at the second plenary meeting of the World Council of Churches held in 1954 at Evanston put two official declarations before the assembly in the last session, read by Michael, Archbishop of America. At this meeting the bishops of the Church of Greece were not present. These declarations made a profound impression on the conference and on the whole Christian world. Shortly after the first of these, if I remember rightly, Michael Ramsey, the then bishop of Durham, now archbishop of Canterbury, took the rostrum and began his address by referring to the Orthodox declaration as "glorious and radical."

The Holy Synod of the Church of Greece held so firmly to its decision, referred to above, that Panteleimon, the metropolitan of Thessalonica, did not venture to take part in the annual meeting of the central committee of the World Council of Churches held in Rhodes in 1959, despite the fact that he was a member of this committee. Many Orthodox and especially Greek members of this committee made a forceful attempt at this meeting to broaden the dogmatic basis of the World Council of Churches, and emphasized that this was a condition *sine qua non* for any further participation of the Church of Greece in the World Council of Churches. Fortunately a *modus vivendi* was arrived at in the annual meeting of the central committee held at St. Andrews, Scotland, in 1960. On the basis of the liturgy of St. John

5. He died in 1950.
6. See Irenaeus of Samos, *Meletemata*, I, 1960; P. Bratsiotis, "The Metropolitan Irenaeus of Samos and the World Council of Churches," in *Ekklesia* 1963, pp. 475–479; D. Savramis, "Ecumenical Problems," in *Kyrios*, 1963.

Chrysostom the following formula was accepted as settling this pressing matter: "The World Council of Churches is a fraternal union of Churches which, according to the Scriptures, recognizes our Lord Jesus Christ as God and savior and strives to follow out its common vocation to the glory of the one God, Father, Son, and Holy Spirit."

Encouraged by this formula, which, however, had still to be definitively approved by the next plenary gathering of the World Council of Churches meeting at new Delhi, the Greek Synod decided, at the request of the World Council, to send four metropolitans and several professors of both national theological faculties to New Delhi. They were, however, given the following guidelines to follow:

1. The unabbreviated form of the trinitarian dogma must be recognized as the basis of the World Council of Churches.

2. There was to be no integration of the Mission Council with the World Council of Churches.

3. The member Churches of the World Council should expressly repudiate any form of proselytizing.

4. They were to insist on an official Orthodox declaration at a plenary assembly of the World Council.

Unfortunately the efforts of the Athens delegation at New Delhi remained without effect.[7] The special Orthodox declaration, which had become almost traditional and mandatory since the Lausanne conference in 1927, could not be fitted into the plenary session but was inserted into the acts of the first section. It was due to this unfortunate circumstance that suggestions apropos the ecclesiological significance of membership in the World Council of Churches made at the meetings held in Montreal and Rochester (summer 1963)[8] came from unofficial or only partially official sources. Hence, from our point of view, the reaction of the Orthodox delegations which decisively rejected these suggestions could not but be welcomed. We can only hope that the burning question of Orthodox participation in the World Council of Churches and its meetings, as well as the question of relations with the Roman Catholic Church, will be thoroughly dealt with in future pro-synods of the Orthodox Church or, better, in a Pan-Orthodox conference.

7. D. Savramis, "Ecumenical Problems," in *Kyrios*, 1963, pp. 152 ff; E. Beauduin, in *Irenikon* I, 1962; H. Le Guillou, in *Istina* III, 1963, pp. 331 ff.

8. D. Strottmann, in *Irenikon*, III, 1963, pp. 368 ff; *Herder Korrespondenz*, October, 1963, pp. 14 ff; November, 1963, pp. 72 ff; *Istina* III, 1963, pp. 338 ff; P. Bratsiotis, in *Ekklesia*, November, 1963, p. 530.

Finally, may I be permitted to put forward my own personal view on the ecumenical movement and the World Council of Churches. I have taken part in this movement since the summer of 1929. From August 3–10 of that year the first conference of Eastern and Western theologians was held under the presidency of the Bishop of Novisad, Irenaeus Ciricius (†1954), in his episcopal palace. Within the framework of the "Organization for Practical Christianity" (usually referred to as "Life and Work") the meeting was arranged by the commission for the ecumenical cooperation of theology professors with the purpose of a collective interpretation of the Epistle to the Philippians. Martin Dibelius, then rector of the University of Heidelberg, chaired the meeting at which the following professors took part: K. Beth, F. Bednasch, H. Clavier, C. H. Dodd, N. Glubokowski, W. Michaelis, K. L. Schmidt, and the author. The second of such conferences took place September 6–12, 1930. At this meeting the Epistle to the Ephesians was interpreted under the presidency of A. Kury, Old Catholic bishop and professor at the Christian-Catholic faculty of the University of Berne. Under the scientific direction of Martin Dibelius the following scholars took part: N. Arseniew, S. Bulgakoff, H. Clavier, B. Gheorghiu, N. Glubokowski, F. Lieb, W. Michaelis, H. Neander, T. Odenwald, L. Pass, K. L. Schmidt, D. Stefanowitsch, S. Zankow, and the author. The interpreter was the unforgettable O. Bauhofer.

On this occasion I had the good fortune to meet once again my former teacher of Leipzig days, Nathan Söderblom, the well-known bishop of Uppsala, and to make the personal acquaintance of Adolf Deissmann and Karl Barth, both famous theologians even at that time.

Later on, during the preparatory work for the Oxford "Life and Work" world conference which was organized by the central office at Geneva, I became an official participant in the ecumenical movement. The regional conferences of the Balkan countries which took place at Herzog Novi (1936) and Novisad (1937) and which dealt with the great theme of the Oxford conference "State–Nation–Church" were part of this preparatory work. I also took part as a member of the Greek delegation in the two world conferences held in 1937, "Life and Work" at Oxford and "Faith and Order" at Edinburgh, and also in the regional conference of the Balkan countries held at Novisad in 1940 during the war, at which W. Visser't Hooft and Eugene Gerstenmaier were also present. The theme of this conference was the situation of the Christian with regard to war, and I presented the Orthodox point of view in a paper on this question.

During the occupation (1941–1944) I was able to keep in touch with the central office in Geneva by means of the Red Cross.

In the summer of 1947 I took part in the preparation for the world conference at Amsterdam at a special meeting called in Geneva, and in the summer of the following year was present at two preparatory conferences held in Holland. Together with several Greek colleagues and Orthodox bishops I represented our Church at the Amsterdam world conference in August, 1948. During all this time I was busy directing the Christian Youth Movement in Greece and even before the war had close contact with the International Union of Christian Students with its headquarters at Geneva.

Together with several of my Greek colleagues I took part in the second plenary assembly of the World Council of Churches held at Evanston in 1954. From 1956 to 1961 I was a full member of the central committee of the World Council of Churches and was chosen to form part of its committee for social work. In this double capacity I took part in conferences held at Herrenhalb, Germany (1956); Nyborg, Denmark (1958); and Rhodes (1959). I was also kept busy in the preparatory work for the conference on the social revolution of our times which the World Council of Churches organized at Thessalonica in 1959 under the presidency of Professor de Vries.[9]

Since 1956 I have been a member of the Greek synodal commission for cooperation with the World Council and for relations with other Churches in general. My name was put forward by the Holy Synod as a member of the Greek delegation at the third plenary assembly of the World Council at New Delhi (1961), but for reasons of health I was unable to take part.

This, briefly, is the history of my own part in the ecumenical movement during the last thirty-four years. These were very valuable years for me, and the experience I gained enabled and even obliged me to draw my own conclusions on what this movement has achieved. The position I take is neither absolutely negative nor positive but nuanced. The ecumenical movement has its good aspects—suffice it to think of all the prejudice, lies, hatred, enmity, and injustice rampant for centuries which it has helped to dissolve; the mutual knowledge it has furthered; the love and cooperation it has fostered among different groups of Christians; the fact that it has brought them so much closer together. I must also think with gratitude of the understanding which

9. An official report of the acts of this important conference was published in English, French, German, and Greek.

the World Council of Churches has shown toward the countries of Orthodox faith and the Ecumenical Patriarchate. Yet sometimes ecumenical work seems to me to be carried on in a rather superficial way, with an enthusiasm which does not take account of the facts of psychology and history. This lack of adequate reflection is responsible for the fact that the results achieved are not proportionate to the amount of energy expended. There are, of course, different points of view: in addition to the more critical and sometimes negative judgments expressed by orthodox and other Christian bodies there are those who hold more conciliatory and positive opinions.

The ecumenical movement has gone through various phases in the course of time. Without a doubt it owes a great deal of its strength to its first enthusiastic leaders. Over the last twenty-five years it has a particular debt to the wisdom, theological knowledge, organizational ability, and diplomatic tact of the well-known Dutch theologian W. Visser't Hooft, who studied under Karl Barth, and to William Temple, the well-known English churchman and theologian, archbishop of York and Canterbury, and originator of the "branch theory" and the doctrine of "comprehensiveness."[10] Visser't Hooft took part with Temple in the organization of the Oxford and Edinburgh conferences, and Temple was, to some extent, responsible for the present form of the World Council of Churches.[11] The organizers of the World Council had set themselves the task of cooperating with all kinds of Christians in bringing about the reunion of the Churches according to the commission of the divine Founder himself (John 17:11–20). But, as was to be expected, this task came up against a rigid and monolithic way of thinking not only among Orthodox and Catholics but also among many Protestants. This was, for example, true of Karl Barth until some short time ago. This also explains why, despite the amalgamation between the two ecumenical organizations "Life and Work" and "Faith and Order," the latter, embodying the dogmatic aspects of ecumenical work, had until about 1960 suffered comparative neglect. This was made the subject of a complaint at a meeting of the central committee in Rhodes in 1959, and fully eleven years after Lund the conference on "Faith and Order" at last met in Montreal in 1963.

In recent years, however, people are still trying to avoid the pain-

10. Died in 1944. According to the "branch theory" the different Churches form as it were branches of one and the same tree.
11. See R. Rouse and S. Neill, *A History of the Ecumenical Movement*, p. 70.

fully difficult discussion of the dogmatic differences between the Churches and are giving preference to easier and more practical ways of circumventing these differences. The so-called ecumenical theology is in vogue which prefers to emphasize the common faith, the consciousness that there is but one Church, the union of all souls in Christ achieved through common liturgies and declarations of solidarity. Especially among Christian youth one hears voices raised in support of full intercommunion. Despite the sharp criticism against this approach heard at the world conference for "Life and Work" (Oxford, 1937) this suggestion keeps on cropping up.[12]

All this implies that ecumenical conferences have some aspects which appear unacceptable from the Orthodox viewpoint, namely, their vague and undefined resolutions in which the element of compromise is too evident, and the tendency, which has been becoming stronger, to put aside official declarations made by Orthodox delegates.

The worst and most dangerous aspect of this question is, however, the fact that the participation of the Orthodox Church in the ecumenical movement—even though officially sponsored—has not been well organized, that there is no real vital interest in this movement, that there has been no collective preparation among Orthodox delegates for dealing seriously with the great problems raised in the different conferences, and, finally, that there is no real contact between the various Orthodox delegations at these ecumenical meetings. We can go further and say that it happens not infrequently that some member Churches have no clear knowledge of what happens at these conferences and what results have come from them.

I myself have grown old in the ecumenical movement and would offer just one piece of advice, namely, to abandon several of the methods used until now and substitute for them another way of working together: by fostering mutual knowledge between the Churches, a common sharing in the spiritual treasures and particular experiences proper to each Church, and growing together in that wisdom which comes from attachment to tradition. From such a meeting between the Churches a loving and sincere form of cooperation could grow which would enable the Churches to engage in common combat against the dangers which beset the world today, especially individualism, materialism, and nihilism. By this means Christian ethical standards and a

12. See the report of Visser't Hooft at the third plenary assembly at New Delhi; also Le Guillou, "Réflexions sur l'Assemblée de New Delhi," *Istina*, III, 1963, pp. 331 ff.

genuine Christian culture could be inculcated and promoted.[13]

The Orthodox Church can learn much from Protestants, both directly and indirectly, concerning what to do and what not to do as regards theological knowledge, pastoral care, preaching, how to organize and run catechetics and missions. There is, in particular, much to learn from the observatories and workshops of the World Council in Geneva. I should add, however, that Protestants ought to be able to learn something from the Orthodox: the treasures of our dogmatic, liturgical, exegetical, and canonical traditions are almost inexhaustible, and the study of the Fathers of the Eastern Church, their ascetical and especially their ecclesiological teaching, ought to bear rich fruit. A reorganization of the World Council of Churches should not be effected entirely according to certain Western ecclesiological models; as long ago as 1959, at the annual meeting of the central committee held at Rhodes, Bishop Otto Dibelius suggested an intensive study of the patristic literature of East and West. I believe that this is one of the most genuine approaches to a true Christian renewal.

The experience of the last decades has also taught us to take a critical attitude toward the ways in which the World Council organizes its activities. The great conferences which are organized, especially by "Faith and Order," are composed of all varieties of Christians and tend to estrange rather than to bring Christians together in common understanding. They should be substituted by smaller conferences constituted of Churches in close proximity, for example, between Orthodox and other Eastern Churches, between Roman Catholic, Orthodox, and Old-Catholic, adding perhaps Lutherans, between Lutherans and other Protestant Churches such as Anglicans and others. It is, moreover, absolutely necessary that at these meetings the representa-

13. While correcting the manuscript for publication, I discovered the following sentence in the *Ecumenical Press Service:* "As the Evangelical Church in Germany had already done, so now the Roman Catholic bishops have decided against common, interchurch liturgies" (No. 12, dated August 4, 1965). In his encyclical of 1951 to the Orthodox Churches the ecumenical patriarch had already forbidden Orthodox to take part in such services, and this decision has never been questioned. In No. 15, dated June 5, 1965, I read the good news that the World Council of Churches and the Roman Catholic Church have formed a committee for the first time for mutual cooperation: "The questions which the working committee is competent to deal with include practical cooperation in charitable, social, and international affairs, setting up theological study-programs on ecumenical questions, problems to do with interchurch relations, and such." What was so much to be desired, and what I had felt would happen, has now, thank God, taken place. The Orthodox reader is bound to recall the encyclical of the ecumenical patriarch issued in 1920.

tives of the Protestant Churches put forward the official belief of their own Church rather than their own personal viewpoints.

BIBLIOGRAPHY

R. ROUSE and S. NEILL, *A History of the Ecumenical Movement*, Philadelphia, 1954; R. SLENCZKA, *Ostkirche und Ökumene*, Göttingen, 1962; H. ALVISATOS, *The Greek Orthodox Church* (in Greek), Athens, 1955, pp. 119 ff; Archbishop GERMANOS of Thyatira, "The Relations between the Orthodox Church and the Other Churches" (Greek), *Ekklesia*, pp. 140–160; B. JOANNIDIS, "Die Beziehungen der Orthodoxen Kirche zu den anderen Kirchen," in *Die Orthodoxe Kirche in griechischer Sicht*, II, pp. 117–143; D. SAVRAMIS, "Ecumenical Problems in the New Greek Theology," *Kyrios*, II, III, 1962–1963; S. ZANKOW, *Orthodoxes Christentum des Ostens*, 1928.

ORTHODOX CHURCH AND ROMAN CATHOLICISM

IT IS NO SECRET that since the eleventh century the relations between the two sister Churches, the Orthodox and Roman Catholic, have not been good. They were at least not such as to correspond to the wishes of their divine Founder. Yet these two Churches have much more in common between themselves than each of them has with the Protestant Churches. This feeling of being so near and yet so far away is felt the more keenly the deeper these Churches get involved in the ecumenical movement. The author, whose sympathy with the Roman Church was stated clearly in the first chapter of this work, has been urging for more than three decades that the two sister Churches should promote unity between themselves by means of meetings between Orthodox and Roman Catholic theologians to engage in the scientific study of theology.[1] Over this period I have never ceased to support projects aimed at this; for example, I have written recommendations to Roman Catholic bishops, professors, and learned institutes on behalf of young Greek theologians desirous of continuing their education in France, Belgium, Germany, Switzerland, and Austria.

Such relations have also been promoted by various representatives of both Churches in different countries, but there was not the proper climate for full-scale, peaceful cooperation. Now, however, such a climate has been created by John XXIII, that good, wise, and truly great pope. We would like to recall here his first pioneering moves in this direction. The first step was the calling of the Second Vatican Council, which in my view was the work of a man endowed with the great virtues of an enthusiastic faith, deep humility, sincerity, and love. The second was the establishment of the Secretariat for Christian Unity, entrusted by that far-seeing man to the tested and experienced rector of the Pontifical Biblical Institute of Rome, Augustin Cardinal Bea.

1. See the letter written by me to the editor of *Pax,* a review published by the Benedictine Priory of Prinknash, Gloucester, England, Vol. 137, January, 1933.

As apostolic nuntio, Archbishop Roncalli—later Pope John XXIII—had the opportunity during his stay in Constantinople, Sophia, and Athens to intervene personally on behalf of the people entrusted to him and thereby to become intimately acquainted with them. When I was general secretary of the Christian Social Union, I had the good fortune and the honor of visiting this genial man in the company of the president of the Union, the professor of medicine Aristotle Kousis, and the vice-president, Dr. P. Poulitsas,[2] during the first terrible winter of the occupation, 1941–1942. We asked him on that occasion to plead with the occupation authorities for a just distribution of food and other necessities among the starving population, and we came away certain that he would do everything in his power on our behalf.

On the occasion of the opening of the Second Vatican Council I had the opportunity of giving interviews to two Catholic newspapers, one in 1960 for *The Life of the Spirit*, published in London, and the second in the following year for *Oriente Cristiano,* published in Palermo. At both of these I expressed the enthusiastic interest of the Greek Orthodox world in the Council. I said to the correspondent of *Oriente Cristiano:* "The Second Vatican Council is an internal event of the Roman Catholic Church, not an ecumenical council as were those of the early Church before the division. This, however, does not mean that other Churches, and in particular the Orthodox Church, are not interested in the themes proposed for discussion and the decisions which are taken. This interest is not just indirect but immediate, a positive interest on the ecumenical rather than the local level since the Council is concerned directly with the question of bringing the Churches together. We hope that it will facilitate this task. Trusting in God and the love of Christ for his followers, trusting also in the insight and experience of the Pope and the Roman Catholic hierarchy, I would express the wish and the hope that the Second Vatican Council, unlike the first in 1870, will contribute to lessening the great difficulties in mutual understanding between the two Churches and create a suitable climate not only for the resumption of good relations between our Churches but also for cooperation with the World Council of Churches." Even before the opening of the Council I saw good reason to look forward hopefully to what it might achieve, and the events of the following years confirmed my optimism.

Together with other members of the special commission established

2. Later president of the State Council and the Greek government.

by the Holy Synod for relations with other Churches, I expressed the view that the invitation sent to us at the prompting of John XXIII by the general secretary of the Secretariat for Church Unity, Cardinal Bea, should be accepted. Our synod would in fact have sent the observers invited to the Council had not unforeseen difficulties prevented the decision from being put into effect. This, however, did not signify that our Church, both its leaders and Orthodox Christians in general, did not follow the work of the Council with great interest. The course of the Council was well documented in our ecclesiastical publications—especially the official church review *Ekklesia*—and the daily press. In addition, many of my colleagues have written studies on various aspects of the Council. All too soon the great efforts of John XXIII for the success of the Council were terminated by his death. Both his last sickness and his death were followed with deep and heartfelt concern not only in the press but throughout the whole Church and the land of Greece. Of particular significance in this regard was the unusual obituary notice which appeared in *Ekklesia:*

After an heroic struggle with death, a struggle which gave the supreme proof of his patience and greatness of soul, Pope John XXIII has departed this life. The death of the greatly esteemed leader of the Roman Catholic Church has left a great gap not only in his own Church but also throughout the whole Christian world. By his efforts the ground has now been prepared for co-operation with other Churches, and, in addition, fruitful contact has been made even with those who would build a world without Christ. Pope John XXIII expressed himself openly and frankly; he associated freely with people, visited the sick and those in prison, and lived a life which was, until then, unthinkable for the head of the Roman Church. It is therefore not difficult to understand how the death of this peace-loving and liberal Pope has caused such deep sorrow throughout the Christian world. We pray that God may be pleased to elevate a worthy successor to the papacy in the place of John XXIII.[3]

I do not know whether such a warmhearted obituary notice has ever appeared in any Orthodox publication since the Schism. At any rate, these words are not only a recognition of and tribute to a great and holy Pope who had something about him of St. Francis of Assisi, but at the same time a sign of the honor in which his Church is held by Orthodox Christians. This sign is an implicit proof of the real sense of solidarity which the Orthodox Church has with her sister Church.

3. *Ekklesia*, May 15, 1963.

The appointment of Cardinal Bea, the well-known Old Testament scholar and former rector of the Biblical Institute of Rome, to the head of the Secretariat for Church Unity, gave me special pleasure. As an Old Testament scholar myself, I had been in correspondence with him even before the Second World War and had in 1951 visited him in the company of my friend Father Joseph Gill, now head of the Oriental Institute in Rome. On that occasion he did me the honor of showing me through the Biblical Institute and its fine library. Full of admiration, I have followed in these last few years his untiring efforts for closer understanding between the Churches and, recently, between the Roman Catholic Church and the World Council of Churches. I was therefore very pleased when the Athenian Academy in its plenary session of May 3, 1965, appointed him one of its associate members.

I had already finished writing this book when an event, for me of worldwide significance, occurred, namely, the meeting between His Holiness Pope Paul VI and the Ecumenical Patriarch Athenagoras. This meeting took place in the country in which Jesus himself had lived, in which he founded the Church, prayed for unity among his followers and all the faithful, in which he gave his blood for the salvation of mankind, was buried and rose again, ascended to heaven, and sent the Holy Spirit. In spite of the fact that progress in general throughout the world had made the task of mutual understanding easier there were still great difficulties to overcome, the more so that, on the Orthodox side, the meeting had not been adequately prepared for and was more in the nature of a spontaneous gesture. The holiness of the place and the prudence and ability of the two high dignitaries made for a meeting of great seriousness and consequence, though this could not disguise the fact that there were difficulties and misunderstanding on both sides, especially in the Orthodox world, as we were to discover in the third Pan-Orthodox Synod of Rhodes. In the first place we have to take account of the fact that the position of the ecumenical patriarch in the Orthodox world is that of *primus inter pares*—the first among leaders of autocephalous Orthodox churches who hold equal jurisdictional rights. This means that the autocephalous Orthodox Churches decide for themselves what their relations with non-Orthodox Churches are to be, and for lack of time the necessary understanding could not be reached before the meeting which took place on January 6, 1964.

To the time of writing there has not been any official declaration emanating from any of the autocephalous Churches on this great and unexpected event, the meeting between the leaders of the two sister Churches. Not even in the above-mentioned Pan-Orthodox Synod of Rhodes was anything said about it. We can, perhaps, attribute this silence to surprise and astonishment, but in any case it cannot detract from the enormous significance of the event. And even if it is interpreted as showing some reservation, it does not affect the closer union between the two sister Churches.

The Orthodox Church has taken part in the World Council of Churches from its inception, and this body is composed, for the most part, of Protestant Churches. My opinion has remained unchanged during thirty-five years that a dialogue between the Catholic and Orthodox Churches should first be organized in an unofficial way, in the same manner as, in the West, Catholic and Protestant theologians first came together in unofficial dialogue. By now this is, thank God, the normal thing. After the Orthodox conference of Rhodes (1963), which decided in the first place for direct dialogue, I am now inclined to favor semiofficial conferences between Roman Catholic and Orthodox experts but do not agree with the suggestion that the World Council of Churches should be brought into this Orthodox-Roman Catholic dialogue. An intervention of the World Council at this point would be both unpractical and uncalled for, since, despite our membership in this body, we would not be obliged to this course and would have to avoid the impression of forming a political alliance; and what kind of ecclesiological agreement could we expect if the Protestant Churches also took part in the dialogue? Any progress in the dialogue within the World Council of Churches presupposes some closer approximation to Orthodox ecclesiology, and this presents far greater difficulties to Protestants than it does to Catholics.

Other events took place in 1964, some of which were bound to increase mutual suspicion between the two Churches, while others on the contrary could serve to improve relations. There was first the invitation of the Pope, made at Bethlehem on the day of the meeting with the Ecumenical Patriarch, to the divided Churches to return to the one fold. This marred the joy felt in the Orthodox world at this historic meeting, and when the invitation was repeated in the encyclical *Ecclesiam Suam* of August 10 it gave rise to negative comments both in the World Council and in the whole Orthodox world. It also affected the feelings of those who took part in the third Pan-Orthodox Synod of Rhodes. Fortunately after these invitations there followed two friendly gestures which went some way toward reassuring people and improved the atmosphere of the Rhodes synod. The first was the quite unexpected greeting sent by the Pope at the opening of the synod, the main theme of which was precisely the question of dialogue with Rome. The other was the festive return of the venerable relics of the blessed Apostle Andrew on his feast day, November 30, 1964, to the church of St. Andrew at Patras. This was brought about by a commission of Roman Catholic clerics with Cardinal Bea at their head.

The Pan-Orthodox synod decided that the dialogue with Rome should be officially inaugurated after the close of the Second Vatican Council, though each autocephalous Church could initiate its own (unofficial) dialogue even earlier.

In the first half of 1965, then, decisive steps toward the Orthodox Church had been taken both by the Roman Catholic Church and the World Council of Churches. On the Catholic side the place of honor has to be given to the first-ever visit of Cardinal Bea to the head-quarters of the World Council in Geneva, the city of Calvin, on February 18 of that year. The cordial way in which he was received, his dialogue with the general secretary and the well-known French pastor M. Boegner, above all, his official declaration that Rome had agreed to the formation of a common working committee, gave great hope of future progress.

There followed the first meeting of the newly formed committee in the ecumenical institute of Bossey near Geneva under the presidency of Monsignor Willebrands and Visser't Hooft, who took the chair in alternative sessions. In the same year the visit of an official Roman Catholic delegation to the Ecumenical Patriarch, with Cardinal Bea at its head, was of considerable importance. We were deeply moved some time later at the expressions of sympathy which were sent by the most ancient of the sister Churches, among those of other Churches, when the Second Rome, its leader, and the faithful were grievously afflicted.

On the other hand, the Church of Greece and the other Orthodox Churches still look forward to the speedy setting aside of the greatest obstacle that stands in the way of the dialogue which is about to begin—I mean the Uniate Church and its unhappy addiction to prose-lytizing. This Church was established in Athens and Macedonia after the disasters of 1922 in Asia Minor but was previously quite unknown in Greece.

In conclusion let us pray that the whole community of Christ, all of whom are baptized in the name of the Father, Son, and Holy Spirit, may through the love of Christ and the assistance of the Holy Spirit find a common ecclesiology based on the Scriptures and the tradition of the primitive Church, so that it may form one Body whose Head is Christ and whose members are all Christians. Then all will be able to drink of the one chalice and partake in the one communion of the Body and Blood of Christ.

God grant that this meeting between the heads of the two sister Churches may be the beginning of a process which leads them closer together and eventually to reunion, as it becomes, in the words of the greeting addressed by our Patriarch to His Holiness, Pope Paul VI, on the vigil of the Epiphany, "the dawn of a blessed day full of light." God grant also that Paul VI may carry on into the future the internal and external ecclesiastical policy of his predecessor and continue that same tactful sensitivity toward and love for the other Churches and all mankind, so that the sister Church of Rome may show forth anew her ancient claim to be προκαθημένη τῆς ἀγάπης ("the foremost in the bond of love"). Our brothers in the West can be sure that the Orthodox Church incessantly prays for the unity of all Christians— ὑπὲρ τῆς τῶν πάντων ἑνώσεως—and strives to come ever closer to all other Churches, above all the apostolic Church of Rome. We believe that the fulfillment of this prayer depends to a great extent on the decisions made at the Second Vatican Council and the way they are put into practical effect.

A LOOK INTO
THE FUTURE

THUS FAR I have dealt with the history and basic characteristics of my revered spiritual mother, the Orthodox Church, and how it stands in relation to the world and other Christian Churches. At this point I would like to go on to express my wishes and hopes for the future. Much of what I will say concerns the Orthodox Church as a whole, but even when I am referring to the Greek Church to which I belong this can be taken as applicable to the entire Orthodox Church.

1. In spite of the fact that Bible reading is widespread in the Orthodox Church, it is still of pressing necessity to spread the Word of God even more and strive for a deeper knowledge of it.[1] Today many editions of the Bible are available in a good translation with introduction and commentary.

2. Likewise, the treasures of patristic literature and hymnography should be much better known than they are. *Apostolike Diakonia* was responsible for the edition of the Fathers of the Church with introduction and an alphabetical index. In addition we need translations of selected patristic texts for use at the popular level.

3. The national church of Greece has always been concerned with the Christian mission to its own people, but in spite of constant religious activity covering a century, which has not been without effect, there is still plenty of room for widening and increasing this internal missionary effort. Great attention must be given to systematic pastoral work, especially in confession, and particular account of the young and those in industry must be taken.

4. Intensive application to the external mission is, and must remain, of primary importance for the Greek Church with its rich missionary tradition. In these last years Africa has opened its doors, and a hopeful beginning has been made in Uganda, Kenya, and Tanzania. The native African communities are under the protection and control of

1. According to the statistical data of the British Bible Society 116,866 copies of the Bible were sold by the office of the Society in Athens during 1962 in either complete or partial editions. In the same year *Zoé* sold 1706 copies of the Greek text of the Old Testament (the Septuagint) and 40,581 Greek New Testaments, while another society, *Sotér*, sold 12,000 copies of the two-volume Greek New Testament with introduction, original text, translation, and notes by Professor P. Trembelas.

the Greek Orthodox Patriarchate of Alexandria. In these parts Greek clerics are working with great zeal side by side with native African theologians who did their studies at the University of Athens. In Athens itself a missionary center has been founded, and in Thessalonica a "Society for the Friends of Uganda."

5. One of the greatest responsibilities of our Church is the preservation of the spiritual health of the people, the young in particular.

6. The question of priestly vocations is intimately connected with this. In present-day society the clergy have a difficult and responsible task. In order that they may remain fully conscious of this, ecclesiastical discipline needs to be strengthened and a spiritual renewal fostered.

7. Our Church gives top priority to a revival and reorganization of monasticism. The great force that monasticism can exert is witnessed by the history of the early Church and succeeding centuries. This inexhaustible source of ecclesiastical and spiritual life must not on any account be neglected, as we can see by what is happening in the Catholic Church and the revival of monasticism in Anglicanism and among the Reformed Churches (for example, Taizé).

8. Another wish of mine for the Orthodox Church is that the rights of the laity should be fully recognized and implemented according to the Scriptures and sacred tradition. The religious revival of the last hundred years has been due principally to the laity. In this respect it is a happy sign that the laity have made so much progress in the strongly hierarchical Roman Catholic Church. In the pronouncements of recent popes and the Second Vatican Council their rights have been emphasized and their cooperation sought to very good effect. The rich experience of the Churches behind the Iron Curtain, especially the Russian Church, is very instructive on the significant role of the laity, and especially of women, in the preservation of faith and church life.

9. Harmonious cooperation between Church and state is very much to be desired, and this can come about only if each respects the sphere of operations of the other. The history of our Church shows that this is possible, since that history has been intimately associated throughout with the history of our people.

10. Our Church must be deeply concerned about social justice and the material and spiritual needs of the people. But this concern, and Christian love in general, cannot be dissociated from social welfare carried out by the state.

11. The Church must be fully engaged in social questions and in

combating the secularizing and anti-Christian tendencies in our society today.

12. In spite of the formidable political difficulties involved, it is the inescapable duty of the Orthodox Church as a whole to promote mutual understanding among the associated Orthodox Churches and work out a definite approach vis-à-vis other Christian bodies. Important steps in this direction were taken at the Pan-Orthodox Synods of Rhodes (1961, 1963, 1964) and the unforgettable gathering of Orthodox leaders at the celebration of the thousandth anniversary of Mount Athos in the summer of 1963. The common spirit and climate of love evident in the Pan-Orthodox conferences will not easily be forgotten by those who took part in them, Orthodox and non-Orthodox. It was something of a new Pentecost. In fact, these synods opened with the Pentecost liturgy, and Byzantine hymns associated with Pentecost were sung at each session—a sign of a really new spirit which was also felt at the Pan-Orthodox celebrations commemorating the first monastic foundation on Mount Athos and which illustrated once again the strong bond of unity existing between the Orthodox Churches. These were surely the most happy events to have occurred since the unfortunate schism of the eleventh century. Between June 22 and 24, 1963, Mount Athos, the great spiritual center of Orthodoxy, witnessed a concelebration in which five patriarchs and the Primate of the Greek Church took part with the Ecumenical Patriarch as principal celebrant. Paul, the only king of Orthodox faith, was also present at the celebrations. Both these events which brought the peoples and Churches of the Orthodox world together in such an unexpected way after centuries of estrangement—they had been united only in faith, liturgy, and a common church government—can be attributed alone to divine inspiration. We are filled with joy and gratitude when we see that Orthodox Christians have in this way made their own contribution to the peace of the world in this precarious age in which we live.

The direct initiative for these events came from the center of Orthodoxy, the Church of Constantinople, a Church which, after a long and glorious history, has been so diminished in recent decades and has had new sufferings heaped on it in the last few years. It has notwithstanding preserved its historic and canonical role in a suspicious and unfriendly milieu, and we hope that, with the help of God, it will continue to do so. The Ecumenical Patriarchate has providentially emerged from these celebrations as having a God-given part to play in the eyes of both Orthodox and non-Orthodox Christians.

The results of these events, however, have still to be worked out and made fruitful on the spiritual and moral planes. The first task is to establish the pro-synod which should play a great part in the future development of the Orthodox Church. All these hopes and desires which I have expressed apply, *mutatis mutandis,* to all the autocephalous Orthodox Churches, in particular the Church of Greece. All of these, together with the Ecumenical Patriarchate, are the immediate descendants of the ancient Greek Church. By God's grace the Greek Church is the largest of the free Orthodox Churches and is keenly aware of her correspondingly great responsibility to the whole Orthodox world.

All the things we desire for the Orthodox Church—both those which I have expressed and others which could be added to them—will, however, remain unfulfilled if we leave out of account the prayer of Christ our Founder and Savior, "that all may be one." The duty is incumbent on us to strive with all our strength to fulfill the task which is implicit in this prayer. A first important step in this direction is the creation of mutual understanding among the Orthodox Churches themselves. This is a condition *sine qua non* for furthering understanding with other Churches. But the basis for any understanding between Churches is in the last analysis that humility and love which our Savior showed forth in his person.

EPILOGUE

Since a Catholic press has kindly put this "pulpit" at my disposal, I feel obliged to emphasize once more the necessity of furthering mutual understanding between the Churches based on mutual love. My text would be from Hebrews 10:24: "let us understand one another and stir one another up to love and good works."

There can be no unity in faith without humility and love. Without these neither Roman Catholic nor Orthodox will be able to make the decisions necessary if there is to be mutual understanding and eventual reunion. This is the message addressed to us by the ancient Church before the schism, and the same message is heard today in the liturgy of St. John Chrysostom just before the recital of the creed: "Let us love one another so that we may live in unity."

FURTHER READING

H. Alvisatos, *Procès-Verbaux du I Congrès de Théologie Orthodoxe,* Athens, 1939.

H. G. Beck, *Kirchliche und theologische Literatur im Byzantinischen Reich,* Munich, 1959.

P. Bratsiotis, *Die Orthodoxe Kirche in griechischer Sicht,* 2 vols., Stuttgart, 1959–1960.

S. Bulgakov, *The Orthodox Church,* London, 1935.

R. M. Dawkins, *The Monks of Athos,* London, 1936.

P. Evdokimov, *L'Orthodoxie,* Paris, 1960.

G. Every, *The Byzantine Patriarchate,* London, 1962 (2nd ed).

G. P. Fedotov, *The Russian Religious Mind,* New York, 1960 (paper-back ed.)

J. Gill, *The Council of Florence,* Cambridge, 1959.

M. J. Le Guillou, *L'Esprit de l'Orthodoxie Grecque et Russe,* Paris, 1961.

F. Heiler, *Urkirche und Ostkirche,* Munich, 1937.

H. A. Hodges, *Anglicanism and Orthodoxy,* London, 1955.

J. M. Hussey, *The Byzantine World,* New York, 1961.

R. Janin, *Les églises orientales et rites orientaux,* Paris, 1952 (2nd ed).

J. Meyendorff, *The Orthodox Church: Its Past and Its Role in the World Today,* New York, 1962.

G. Ostrogorsky, *History of the Byzantine State,* New Brunswick, N. J., 1957

L. Ouspensky and V. Lossky, *The Meaning of Icons,* Boston, 1956.

M. Rinvolucri, *Anatomy of a Church: Greek Orthodoxy Today,* London, 1966.

B Rouse and S. C. Neill, *A History of the Ecumenical Movement,* London, 1954.

S. Runciman, *The Eastern Schism,* Oxford, 1955.

P. Sherrard, *The Greek East and the Latin West,* London, 1959.

N. Zernov, *The Russians and Their Church,* London, 1945.

INDEX